SIGNED COPY

SCENES FROM THE P

LANCASHIRE CANAL CARRIERS

J. MONK & SONS

Twenty Steps Lock, Manchester Ship Canal/Runcorn & Latchford Canal, April 1961. Having worked transhipment loads down from Ellesmere Port, whilst traffic on the MSC was restricted following the sinking and later salvage of the *SS Mary P Cooper,* the Monk boats *Irwell* and *June* leave the ship canal bound for Warrington's Howley Quay. *Irwell* has already been worked through and Jim Monk Jnr takes a line from Tommy Cullen, *June's* skipper, and drops it over a bollard to secure *June* before closing the bottom gates. The lock parapet is fouled by detergent foam which also pollutes the water. ***Norman Jones***

NORMAN JONES

JAMES MONK JNR & LEONARD MONK

SIGNED COPY

£15

Copyright © Foxline and Norman Jones
ISBN 1-870119-54-1
All rights reserved
Designed and Edited by Gregory K. Fox,
Norman Jones and Paul Shackcloth.
Typeset by Norman Jones and Paul Shackcloth
Printed by: Amadeus Press, Huddersfield

Published by Foxline
32 Urwick Road, Romiley, Stockport SK6 3JS

ACKNOWLEDGEMENTS & ABOUT THIS BOOK

Publication of my article "AROUND THE BLACK BEAR" (Waterways World May 1990) featuring Mr J. Monk Jnr. of Adlington, with the short boats *Irwell* and *June,* led to this book about the Lancashire based canal carrying firm, and the waterways where they operated. Over a span of seven years the work has been rewritten and revised to keep abreast of current events. The MSC road bridges are now only manned 'as required' yet in 1998 we had the Inland Waterways Association Annual Festival & Inland Boat Show at Salford Quays, with 300 boats in Huron Basin (the old No 9 Dock) of hallowed memory; there was an inspiring IWACC report on restoration priorities, the prospect of the Huddersfield Narrow Canal being re-opened, progress on the Rochdale Canal front and the Ribble link project. Alan Meale MP, the Waterway Minister has announced some increased funding for British Waterways, with promises of some resurgence of commercial carrying, whilst full restoration of the Anderton Boat Lift now seems assured. In a nationwide consultation launched by British Waterways, the general public as well as users of BW river and canal navigations have been asked for their views on a proposal for a national membership scheme, allied to a new charitable trust. A copy of the consultation document "Partnership with the People" is available from BW Customer Services Dept, or local BW waterway offices. Details are also available at a BW Special website.

In writing this book I have had Jim Monk's recollections on tape, his sons Leonard and Ian have found family snapshots and helped with research, as has Leonard's wife Ann. Photographs and information have freely been made available by: Harry Arnold, Waterway Images; Irlam historian and photographer Jim Ashton and son Donald Ashton, an expert on MSC tugs; Michael and Chris Bentley; Gordon Biddle, a doyen of railway as well as waterway history; Lynn Doylerush, Archive Officer at the Boat Museum, Betty M. Buckley and Ron Tinker, Rochdale Canal Society; Suzanne Cameron, Preston Marina; Jean & Paul Doran of "The Liverpool Boat" - Burscough II," Chris Topp (June) Carlton Husthwaite, Thirsk, N. Yorks, Donna O' Keefe, Trafford Park Development Corporation, Wayne & Debbie Davies, Warrington historian David Fance, Ted Gray, highly respected writer on MSC and waterway matters, Jean, Amy and John Lawless, John was employed in Cooper's office at the time of the Mary P. Cooper incident and shared his personal knowledge of Cooper ships with me. Peter Hobart keeps me abreast of current transport events on land or sea and fellow author Eddie Johnson is always on the look-out for items of shipping interest. Another valued friend Mrs Nell Round, has provided the material on past decades of her home town Wigan and the L&L Canal and thanks to Lisa Holdsworth, Production Co-ordinator, Screenhouse Productions Ltd, Leeds (BBC 5 History Fix) for the interest in Monk's' June. Always ready to assist my good friends Jim Peden 'Photographs of Transport & Industrial History' and John Ryan have put their picture libraries at my disposal. David Lowe of Apollo Cruises, Shipley who acquired some of the Monk Boats when that family retired from commercial boating has been unstinting in providing information and photographs. I am also indebted for information and comment to WE (Bill) Leathwood, former ICI Northwich Shipping Manager and authority on Mersey Flats, and Karl Moston, currently with a narrow-boat on the Bridgewater Canal at Lymm, sadly his Dad and my long-time friend Donald Moston, who knew all about the Massey Brook Canal Arm is no longer with us. Sincere thanks also to AJ (Tony) Robinson - and son Liam - who have contributed current ship canal photographs; thanks to J Rutherford, Assistant to Port Director c/o The Manchester Ship Canal Co, Port Division, Runcorn WA7 1HA for photographic permits and C Ashton and W Cavanagh at Ellesmere Port Docks for their courtesy and co-operation during Tony's visits. Thanks also for the loan of Ship Canal artefacts to Carolyn Carr and her Mum, the late Mrs Rita Gallimore (who sadly never got her copy of this book). From his documentary record come Keith Hodgkinson's pictures of the Centenary Bridge at Trafford Park. We have tried to identify all picture sources, but must also acknowledge the unidentified photographers whose prints are credited as 'Authors' or 'L Monk collection'. As always the support, and advice of Greg Fox (Foxline) and his wife Jacqueline has been invaluable, whilst the publishing expertise of Richard Cook, David Crossland and all at Amadeus Press is unsurpassed. Very few photographers captured Monk boats at work, but the contemporary pictures chosen here do reflect the locations and scenes that were familiar to Mr J Monk Snr, and his sons during their lifetime on the canals of Lancashire.

Readers will appreciate that all references to waterways, canals, locks, basins, routes, etc, form part of the narrative only and should not be used for route planning or as an aide to navigation.

NJ©

Nr.Worsley (Patricroft Hospital Centre.) Mon 17 July 1961. Skipper John Mailey has loaded Monks' *Jean* at Boothstown and is now heading for either the Barton or Trafford Park Power Station. The boat *Jean* had recently been repainted at the Worsley Boat Yard and, looking very smart and tidy, is seen to be carrying a different style of lettering to others of the fleet. Repair work is being effected at the hospital and 'period' atmosphere is enhanced by the corrugated iron fencing. Right, the smart Ford Consul car and the 'corner shops' observed in the rows of terraced housing.

H.Arnold (Waterway Images)

INTRODUCTION

Monk's of Adlington, Lancashire, were established members of the working boat fraternity on the Leeds & Liverpool, Bridgewater and Manchester Ship Canals from the 1930's until commercial carrying on those inland waterways ended in the late 1960's, early 1970's.

The canal age and Britain's industrial revolution went hand-in-hand in the second half of the eighteenth century, when working folk began to move from their traditional occupations in agriculture and cottage industries to form an urban population engaged in mills and factories, living under the control of industrial capitalists rather than hereditary landowners, but signs of change had been evident from the beginning of the period.

In the latter years of the seventeenth century, Thomas Steers, an engineer with a military background, had worked with George Sorocold on plans for the construction of the Howland Great Wet Dock at Rotherhithe, opened in 1699 and Steers' scheme for Liverpool's first dock (for which an Act was secured in 1709) was accepted in preference to that proposed by his colleague, Sorocold.

Thomas Steers was also active in riparian work in the North-west and in 1712 both surveyed and provided plans for the Mersey & Irwell and River Douglas Navigations; the latter made navigable by 1740 from Miry Lane, Wigan, to Parbold, Tarleton and the Ribble estuary, was purchased by the Leeds & Liverpool Canal company in 1772, an astute move, as the navigation owned the headwaters of the river and consequently a water supply which was essential to the success of the Leeds & Liverpool undertaking.

Since it was authorised in 1770, built in somewhat piece-meal fashion (at a cost of around £1,200,000), with its main line from Leeds to Liverpool not complete until 1816, (and then only by virtue of a 'sharing agreement' with the Lancaster Canal Company of the stretch that runs from Wigan Top Lock to the Bottom Lock of Johnson's Hillock), it is difficult to define a 'Bi-Centenary' or other notable date for Britain's longest canal (127 miles excluding branches), built by one body, the Leeds & Liverpool Canal Company.

However, specific dates can be quoted in the case of the Mersey & Irwell Navigation, (opened from the Runcorn Gap via Warrington through to Manchester by 1734), the Bridgewater Canal (opened to Runcorn by 1776) and the Manchester Ship Canal (1894). Nowadays pleasure craft have replaced working boats on the broad but comparatively shallow L&L and Bridgewater canals, whilst essential if rigorous regulations including a requirement for substantial third-party insurance and VHF radio preclude their casual entry onto the Manchester Ship Canal, built for the passage of ocean going ships.

Some official 'NOTES ON THE PORT OF MANCHESTER' dated April 1953 stated : "DIMENSIONS - Depth. The Canal is constructed to give normally an available depth of 30ft. from Eastham to Ince Oil Berth 5 miles; and of 28ft from Ince to Manchester Docks".

Over the last two decades the focus of commercial traffic on the Manchester Ship Canal has been directed largely to the lower reaches of the undertaking between Eastham, Ellesmere Port, Stanlow and Runcorn, rather than towards the Mode Wheel and Salford Quays, Trafford Park and the main dock systems, whilst the former Manchester Dock estate, no longer frequented by shipping, has been revitalised as the Salford Quays development, which includes prestigious business, residential, hotel and leisure projects.

The once busy docks where Jim Monk Snr and his sons, their friend, Albert Blundell and others plied their trade are now 'water parks', whilst new 'ornamental style' canals as opposed to commercial waterways link the former docks, overlooked by impressive but non-maritime oriented new buildings. No 7 Dock is now a venue for anglers, having been stocked with fish by Salford City Council; there is an area known as 'Harbour City' around the old No 9 Dock; and radio controlled model boats have replaced commercial traffic in the former No 8 Dock, renamed 'Ontario Basin.'

The names chosen for the new water features are a reminder of Manchester Liners, a company whose fine fleet of cargo liners and later generation of purpose built container carrying vessels were an object of civic pride - and commemorate their trade links with ports on the shores of the Great Lakes of North America, indeed they were the first British Company into the Lakes, had the first ship into the St Lawrence Seaway, operated the first British deep-sea container service and gained a Queen's Export Award.

On the 17th July 1961, the Manchester Ship Canal Co, the proprietors of the Bridgewater Canal celebrated the bi-centenary of the crossing by the first coal laden boat from Worsley, of James Brindley's famous stone Aqueduct, which carried the Duke's new navigation across the River Irwell at Barton. The historic Bridgewater Canal, (in the vernacular 'Duke's Cut') was conceived by Francis, the 6th Earl and 3rd Duke of Bridgewater (1736-1803), solely to serve his mines at Worsley.

The works were executed under the direction of self-taught engineer James Brindley (1716-1772); it is now believed that John Gilbert (1724-1795), who was a brother to Thomas Gilbert, the Duke of Bridgewater's Agent at Worsley, had a hand in much of the preparatory work entailed in surveying the route, and undertook some of the day to day supervision of the excavations.

By the end of 1761 the 'Navigation' was opened throughout from the Duke's coal mines at Worsley to Stretford, from where coal was taken on to Manchester by horse and cart; extra toll gates were placed along the road taken by the carts to ensure that the Duke paid the necessary turnpike tolls, a situation that existed until 1764 when the canal reached Castlefield. As work proceeded on the Worsley cut, a route through Cheshire was being surveyed and an Act for the Duke's canal to continue from Stretford, to join the River Mersey at Hempstones near Runcorn, was passed on 24th March 1762; the extension was opened in 1776.

The last Act of Parliament promoted by the Duke was passed in 1795, and was for an extension of the canal westwards from Worsley to Leigh, where an end-on connection would be made with the Leigh branch of the Leeds & Liverpool canal, which left the L&L main line at Wigan.

continued on page 7

Latchford

22 June 1989. The 'stopped off' site of what was originally Latchford Lock (later re-named Manor Lock when the Manchester Ship Canal was built) is seen from the north bank of the River Mersey. The infilled route of what was formerly a section of the Runcorn & Latchford Canal between this point and the also infilled Twenty Steps Locks at Stockton Heath, regularly traversed by working boats like Monks' *June* and *Irwell* in the 1960's is now the Blackbear Linear Park; some of the former canal artefacts, the former swing bridge and remains of the gates have been retained and a plaque close to the bridge gives a brief account of the history of the early navigation.

Norman Jones

Mersey & Irwell Navigation: Stickens Lock 11th October 1890. Built c.1720 and one of eight locks, each 68ft long by 16ft wide, with chambers of massive stone blocks, having strong, but clumsy double gates with heavy balance beams. It was rebuilt to the same dimensions a century later, when bends and deviations in the Rivers Irwell and Mersey were straightened out. The photograph shows the merging of the old navigation with the course of the new Manchester Ship Canal. The lock would seem to then be still operable, possibly only to control water levels - despite being spanned by the trestle bridge carrying the contractor's railway. Trains were controlled by the signal (right) and the two officials or engineers posing for their picture appear in other scenes taken along this 'Stickens' section of the works.
James Ashton Collection

James Brindley's Aqueduct at Barton. c.1890. "An Act to enable the Most Noble Francis, Duke of Bridgewater, to make a navigable Cut or Canal" received Royal Assent on 23 March 1759; Parliament agreed to a change of route in 1760 and Brindley, when questioned in the House about his proposed aqueduct, explained his ideas with a model in cheese. The structure opened on 17 July 1761 included stop boards at each end for use when repairs were needed and 'sluices' to discharge water contained between the 'stops' into the river below. Before a large gathering His Grace the Duke of Bridgewater together with the Earl of Stamford saw the water turned into the Cut and a barge carrying upwards of 50 tons was then towed along the new part of the Canal and over the arches across the River Irwell.
Author's Collection

Barton MSC Canal Aqueduct. c.1895 Where the Bridgewater Canal crossed the new waterway, Brindley's three arch structure was replaced by a swing aqueduct with two moveable spans of 90ft each carrying a waterway 19ft wide and 6ft deep; the canal waterway of the old brick and stone aqueduct, was 18ft wide and 4ft 6in deep. Watertight iron swing gates are fitted at each fixed shore end of the new structure, and also each end of the iron trough. When all four gates are open barges may pass freely along the Bridgewater Canal (a horse-boat is seen crossing) and the gates are closed when the aqueduct has to be swung to allow ships to pass along the Manchester Ship Canal.
Author's Collection

(Top left) Barton Swing Aqueduct. ND. The aqueduct with temporary structures affixed to facilitate access by workmen. The success of the Anderton Lift on the Weaver Navigation, that utilized hydraulic power to lift boats 51ft vertically while floating in an iron trough, suggested to Sir E Leader Williams, the MSC's Chief Engineer, that the same idea might be used for a swing viaduct.
J Ashton Collection

(Top right) Barton Swing Aqueduct 1956. Having loaded at Boothstown on the Leigh arm of the Bridgewater Canal, Albert Blundell's *Finch* tows their dumb boat *Norman* over the aqueduct laden with coal for Stretford Power Station. ***L Monk Collection***

(Bottom left) 'Adjustments' By today's thinking, working conditions were hazardous, witness the vertiginously balanced ladder to the upper girders; on the walkway by the 2nd vertical, one artisan is squeezing through the rails, assisted by another man with a rope over his shoulder. Left foreground lie two screw jacks and a number of large threaded tie bolts and nuts; behind the aqueduct, centre, works a self-propelled steam crane.
Author's Collection

continued from page 4

The success of the new canal hastened the industrial growth of Manchester, Salford and their environs, but it became apparent that improvements made to the route of the tortuous Mersey & Irwell Navigation between Manchester and Warrington, particularly in eliminating notorious bends, such as those at the 'Hell-hole' Latchford, and at Butchersfield near Rixton Leys, were insufficient to enable the waterway to cope with increased traffic.

Two abortive 'ship canal' schemes were aired as far back as the 1840's, but it was not until 1882 that a provisional Manchester Ship Canal Committee meeting at the Didsbury home of Daniel Adamson, initiated a process which culminated in the promotion and construction of the Manchester Ship Canal between 1887 and 1893. This was a prodigious undertaking even by today's standards, and the works partly obliterated the course of the old eighteenth century Mersey & Irwell Navigation, and truncated its Runcorn & Latchford Canal which, opened in 1804 enabled the 'Mersey flats' e.g. sailing barges, to bye-pass the difficult passage of the tidal River Mersey encountered below the first lock of the M&I Navigation, known as Howley or Warrington Lock.

Under the terms of the 3rd Duke of Bridgewater's will, following his death in 1803 the canal and mines were run by a trust until 1845, when the Mersey & Irwell Navigation was merged with the Bridgewater concern. In 1874 the Bridgewater Navigation Co., Ltd., was formed and this company purchased the shares of both of the waterway undertakings from the Trustees for £1,120,000 and in 1885, under the terms of the first Manchester Ship Canal Act, the Bridgewater Navigation Company sold the whole of their properties to the new concern for £1,710,000. The year 1994 commemorated the centenary of the Manchester Ship Canal, which opened to general traffic on the 1st January 1894, when 76 vessels, (headed for the latter part of the passage by the steam yacht *Norseman,* owned by Manchester Ship Canal Director Samuel R. Platt, and carrying Directors, Officials and Dignitaries, who joined the procession at Latchford), left Eastham Locks bound for Manchester's new terminal docks. Queen Victoria performed the official opening ceremony on Monday the 21st May 1894.

In 1961 however Manchester's status as a port remained high, despite some reduction in the volume of trade. Cargo liners, coasters, and tankers regularly made the 35.5 mile passage from Eastham Locks to Manchester, whilst the adjacent waterways were thronged with barge and narrow boat traffic servicing the docks complex. Some of these craft were owned by the MSC and their Bridgewater Department, others by carriers (officially known as 'bye-traders', such as Monks of Adlington, and Albert Blundell of Chorley), all then long established in shipping and inland waterway circles, but many no longer in business due to the decline in Britain's status as an economic and maritime power.

However in 1994, the Ship Canal's Centenary Year, the upper reaches saw more activity, for the maize traffic, which the Monk boats particularly June and Irwell once off-loaded from ocean going vessels at Ellesmere Port for trans-shipment to Manchester was, in compliance with European Common Market

continued on page 12

Barton Locks MSC, Friday 14 April 1893. Replacing the Stickens and Barton Locks of the Mersey & Irwell Navigation, comparison of this picture with that on Page 5 indicates the scale of the new works. The 'large' lock is 600ft x 65ft, the 'small lock' 350ft x 45ft, rise 15ft. By Saturday, 25 November 1893, the MSC was filled throughout, and the Directors made their first full length passage on Thursday, 7 December 1893. Stoney sluices, 30ft wide, constructed parallel to the lock, maintained flood control. Of the four Barton sluices (right) it was stated that one gate weighing fifty tons. could be raised four feet by one man in one minute, using Sir W G Armstrong's hydraulic apparatus. The width of the canal at this point is 330ft.

James Ashton Collection

Mersey & Irwell Navigation. Stickens Old Lock. Wednesday, 11 September 1889. Engineer Thomas Steers, completed Liverpool's first dock in 1715, became Dockmaster in 1716, reclaimed land around the area for building and became involved with three early river navigations, the Mersey & Irwell, the Weaver and the Douglas. Steers surveyed the rivers to Manchester in 1712. The first Mersey & Irwell Company was formed in 1714, an enabling Act was passed in 1721 but the navigation was not opened to Manchester until 1734, with locks at Howley, (Warrington), Millbank (Partington), Calamanco (Flixton), Hulmes Bridge, Stickings (or Stickens), Barton, Mode Wheel and Throstlenest, very much to Steers' original plan. The locks were 68ft long x 16ft wide and the rise at Stickings was 4ft 4ins. This lock was rebuilt, with the same rise, c.1820, however much of the course of the rivers Mersey & Irwell was to be engulfed by construction works for the new Manchester Ship Canal c.1889. This upstream view shows excavations and infilling undertaken to direct the new Manchester Ship Canal along the former bed of the Navigation. Temporary rail tracks abound whilst the two heaps of dressed stone blocks close to the former 'swing bridge' form the nucleus of a supply depot for the new Barton Locks.

NJ from the J Ashton Collection

Mersey & Irwell Navigation. Monday, 20 Jan 1890. Draining the bed of the Irwell at Stickens. A superb posed documentary shot, imagine that intrepid photographer setting up his 10" x 8" stand camera amongst all that mud and debris! Water is being siphoned from the river bed and in the forefront lies a workman's basket containing clothes amidst a jumble of debris and discarded tools in front of the typical contractors side-tipping wagon. Note the chain coupling and pair of sprags through the offside front wheel to secure it in position. The CWS Irlam Soap Works Railway bought one of these wagons from the Ship Canal Co, in 1910 for £12.10.0 (£12.50) it was still giving good service in 1960. Although Steam Navvies were in use, much reliance was placed on manpower, 17,000 men being employed, deployed in eight companies, each responsible for a section of about four miles. The men lived with their wives and families in wooden 'settlements' with reasonable facilities at several points along the canal's route.

NJ from the J Ashton Collection

(Above) Barton Locks/Sluices, Manchester Ship Canal. Wednesday 17 August 1890. A cleverly posed scene at a typical canal construction site. Note the sheeted cement wagon on the contractor's railway, and the partially uncovered stack of bags alongside, also the attitudes struck by the bowler-hatted foremen and the counter-weight on the driving platform of the steam crane. **(Below) Friday 25 November 1890.** This desolate scene is of the same site (Barton) following disastrous floods, when a thirteen mile stretch of the partly constructed canal was inundated. ***James Ashton Collection***

(Above) Bridgewater Canal. The Watch House, Stretford. Saturday, 21 April 1962. Lifeboat conversions on the Cruising Club moorings and the 'leccy' pylons confirm the period. The cemetery is still extant, but sleek Metrolink trams have long since replaced the green liveried slam-door' Manchester-Altrincham electric' trains. Billie Wells' 'own' boat *Hopewell,* seen here, was a former steamer motorised in 1955, and owned by T&W Wells Ltd, who operated Rathbone Brothers Stretford Boatyard. The Watch House is located 4 miles from Castlefield Junction.

H Arnold (Waterway Images)

(Left) c.1950. L&LCanal. Skipper Ernie Parkinson keeps an eye on the photographer whilst working Dean Waddington's *Elsie* up the Wigan flight of locks. ***L Monk Collection***

Manchester Docks (MSC) c.1913. A busy scene at No 8 Dock, with Trafford Wharf seen beyond. Three steamers load for Bombay, as a Watson boat from the 'Med' discharges and a Lamport & Holt cargo liner loads for New York, (5th and 20th of each month) sporting its blue funnel, with broad white band and black top, its identity further established by the house flag with its horizontal bands of red, white, red, with a black L + H on the white band. At this time Messrs Lamport & Holt, with offices at London, Manchester and Liverpool owned 48 steamers of tonnages ranging from 1,994 gt to 6,000 gt, (the latter building). offering services to the River Plate, and Brazil as well as European destinations. Egyptian, or Galveston cotton comprises the rail traffic in the foreground, a load of pit props is being cleared, and (right) an MSC railway dock shunting tank is hard at work.
James Ashton Collection

Trafford Wharf, Saturday 25 August 1956. The railway swing bridge over the MSC. The bridgeman, who has a train halted on the northern bank waiting to cross, regards the progress of an outward bound coaster from the Pomona Docks. The smartly kept, 384 grt *Julia Mary* carrying a deck cargo of commercial vehicles is representative of the smaller ships that maintained the European services. Official Call Sign, PFFB, her Navigational Aids comprised Direction Finder, Echo Sounding Device, Radio Telephone and Magnetic Compass. Built in April 1949, to ✠100A1 Lloyd's Classification by Scheeps "Westerbrook" in the Netherlands, her Port of Registry was Rotterdam and her owners and managers were Slavenburg & Huyser N.V. A 'Machinery Aft' vessel, she measured 181ft 10in x 28ft 7in x 10ft and was powered by an 8 cylinder Werkspoor Oil Engine.
Norman Jones

Salford Quays Development 1993. Messrs Butler & Co., of Leeds built Railway Swing Bridge No 1 which carried a single line over the MSC between Salford yard and Trafford Wharf and was in use from 1895 until 5 April 1943, when it was replaced by the double track swing bridge, (above centre and left) Following the closure and redevelopment of Manchester Docks, the bridge has been moved from its former location and fixed to span the 'old' No 9 Dock, separating the newly named 'Huron Basin' from 'Erie Basin', providing pedestrian acess from the prestigous residential property on the left, to 'Harbour City' on the other side, where commercial office developments are situated. ***Ted Gray***

continued from page 7

regulations being shipped via France to Trafford Park by vessels such as the smart and well-found medium tonnage motor ships of the Arklow Shipping company. The generations of working boatmen and their families, by force of circumstance and situation, lived and worked in closed communities corresponding to those of the railwaymen, and practiced similar qualities of self-reliance, a family stability based on continuity of traditions and a way of life handed down through generations, traits which added much to the British psyche and brought the nation robustly through two World Wars.

J. MONK & SONS OF ADLINGTON, LANCS.

Amongst the officially listed 'Carriers by Water' on the Manchester Ship Canal, its Bridgewater Division and connecting Navigations in the 1950/60's, were British Waterways, North Western Division, Lime Street, Liverpool, and their Northern Fleet Control Office, at Lightbody Street in the same city, the Southern Fleet Control Office, Anderton Lift, Nr. Northwich, and notable private carriers such as Albert Blundell - Chorley, Jonathan Horsefield Ltd - Runcorn, James Monk of Adlington, Lancs, J. Parkes & Sons Ltd - Liverpool, Gordon H. Waddington - Atherton, and T&W Wells, Longford Dry Docks, Stretford, Manchester.

The business later known as J Monk & Sons was started by Mr. J. Monk Snr. who in the early 1930's owned and worked a small Level Adit or Day (Coal) Mine, close to the village of Aberdeen, near to Haigh, on the former South Lancaster Canal length of the L&L canal.

The hard-won coal - there were no mechanical aids other than pick and shovel - was loaded into a horse-drawn 62ft x 14ft 4ins short-boat from which it was bagged and sold to folk inhabiting the small hamlets and canal side cottages in and around Adlington; the boatmen working that length were commonly known as 'Haigh Cutters' from their association with coal mining. The area is steeped in history, for the derivation of the name 'Haigh' is from an old Anglo-Saxon word meaning 'enclosure'; the history of 'Haigh Hall' and its Lord of the Manor dates back to those heroic times. The present day Haigh Hall stands on the site of a pre-Tudor Mansion, which was rebuilt between 1830 and 1849, and supervision of the picturesque building and its extensive grounds is now undertaken by the Leisure Department of the Metropolitan Borough of Wigan; its parklands provide recreational facilities for the 306,000 population of the borough.

On leaving school, Mr J Monk Snr's eldest son Wilfred took a clerical job in the offices of Leyland Motors Ltd., but preferring the more active life of the waterways (around which he had spent most of his formative years) left his sedentary job some 12 months later to go as 'mate' to his dad, who by then was working a horse boat for T&W Wells on the Leeds & Liverpool Canal. A monthly job on which the two young boys often went with their Dad, introduced them to waterway life and gave them an early experience of working boats. Having travelled down the L&L canal from their home at Adlington, with the 62ft wooden horse-boat *George,* the trio took on a load of household coal at the Edge Green Colliery tip and proceeded down the $7\frac{1}{4}$ mile long Rufford Branch, entered then as now, by turning off the 'main line' of the L&L just east of Burscough.

The 'Ship' public house by the second lock up the branch, although now extended and modernised continues, as it did in the 1930's, to offer hospitality to all comers. The working boatmen knew the 'pub' as 'The Blood Tub', as the landlord made and sold a scrumptious Lancashire 'black pudding' the principal constituent of which was the porcine variety of the 'vital fluid'; the branch which replaced the earlier River Douglas Navigation, (closed in 1781) was known simply as 'The Tarleton Line'. Even then the branch was badly silted and shallow, the principal traffic comprising

Twenty Steps Lock and Northwich Road Swing Bridge, MSC. March 1961. Seven swing bridges, similar in appearance but not dimensions, cross the ship canal, that at Stockton Heath, near Warrington, with a clear span of 120 ft is one of the heaviest at 1,083 tons. They were designed to carry a moving load of 40 tons, and dead load of 120 lbs per square foot of road surface. Beneath the massive girders, Jim Monk and Tommy Cullen report to the bridgeman, as Monks' *Irwell,* laden with aluminium ingots transhipped at Ellesmere Port, enters the Runcorn & Latchford Canal, bound for Manor Lock, the River Mersey and Howley Quay. It was a Saturday afternoon and Jim and his Mate intended leaving *Irwell* and *June* moored securely at the Quay over the week-end, as they travelled home to Adlington overland.
Norman Jones

mostly of empty boats passing between the main line and Mayor's Yard at Tarleton before and after repair. The shallow depth of course entailed the boat being hauled slowly and steadily, furthermore the towpath was practically non-existent, so the horse pulling Monks' *George* was forced to pick its way along the edge of the fields which fringed the canal. When he was available, Mr Monk hired an old horse named 'Barney' from a Wigan horse dealer for this job, Barney was a good worker, but took things calmly as befitted his age and his plodding, unhurried pace was ideally suited to pulling a laden short boat along the peaceful length of the Rufford Branch.

The coals taken on at Edge Green were assorted types of household coals, Best House grade, Big and Medium Cobbles, Nuts, etc., amounting to about 38 tons in all, not a full load for the *George* but as much as the available depth allowed.

The coal merchant's house (still extant) and yard were on the bank-side close to Tarleton village, owing to the shallow depth the boat had to lie about 5 yards off the bank, the boys helped their Dad to carry every piece of the 'Big Cobs off by hand, across a narrow gang-plank after which the 'loose stuff' was wheeled off in 3 cwt capacity barrows trundled along the same cat-walk.

Adlington being a canal based community, many of the men-folk worked on the L&L and the village lads were always 'hanging about the boats'. Of many boyhood memories Mr J. Monk Jnr, recalls one typical Saturday afternoon when he was about twelve years old walking with a friend along the canal from Adlington, and down the Wigan flight to the bottom lock, ('Railway Lock'), to meet Tommy Moss, an old boatman who lived at Botany Bay near Chorley. Tommy and his mate worked *Margaret* one of Dean Waddington's square stern horse-boats; the boys' job was to close the lock gates after the *Margaret* had entered, and give a hand generally; in return they got to ride on the boat in between times. It was about four o'clock in the afternoon when they met their friend and about 8 o'clock at night when they got home.

UNDER A BOMBER'S MOON

When Jim Monk left school, trade was quiet on the waterways, so he took a job with the Co-op Bakery at Adlington, but World War II had just started, and the canals were coming into their own again, as fuel rationing restricted the use of motor vehicles, whilst munitions took priority over other classes of rail traffic. Air Raid Precautions were enforced, identity cards were issued as were civilian gas-masks, both items to be carried at all times. To minimise the effect of possible breaches in the canal banks that might be caused by bomb damage, arrangements were made to enable stop planks to be installed at strategic points along the length of the canal. ARP wardens were shown how to use the planks, which at first were put in place every night, and corrugated iron sheeting, sandbags and other materials suitable for sealing breaches were held in readiness. Air raid shelters were erected and examples of the defensive concrete tank traps, block houses, and gun emplacements which dotted the countryside generally became a part of the waterway landscape.

Bisecting the country, and running from east to west, the line of the Leeds & Liverpool canal was considered to be of great strategic importance, as forming a natural line of defence in the event of a retreat by our armies in the face of a successful and overwhelming invasion by the Nazi forces. Terminating as it then did in Liverpool Docks, the Leeds & Liverpool canal suffered as a result of enemy action, particularly during the September 1940 Blitz on Merseyside, when the Nazi bombers also found their way to Leigh, and again during 1941, when the terminal locks and buildings were unusable for some months due to enemy action, and an administrative centre for the canal was set up on the outskirts of the city.

In the first months of the conflict dubbed 'the phoney war', the country gained valuable time in which to move the re-armament programme into high gear. Ever more traffic, particularly of bulk loads was shifted from road hauliers to the waterways and

Near Dean Lock, Wigan. H&R Ainscough's *Parbold* on the 'coal run' to their mills at Burscough and Parbold, was the last working horse boat on the L&L Canal when 'pensioned off' in 1960. The approach to Dean Locks through the pretty Douglas Valley is flanked by the river on one side and the Wigan to Southport railway line on the other, but today the scene is dominated by the massive M6 motorway viaduct. The original lock (which was doubled along with several others in the middle of the last century when coal traffic to Liverpool was heavy) dates back to 1781 and between 1774 and the former date, a river lock, the site of which can still be seen gave access to the River Douglas Navigation.
Harry Arnold Photography

Jim Monk was soon able to leave his bakery job and join his Dad, Mr J Monk Snr (as he was always known) and elder brother Wilfred, who were still working J & W Tomlinson of Blackburn's horse-boats on the Leeds & Liverpool canal. Jim Monk was 17 years old when he 'went on the boats', but 'did his stint' of the arduous pick and shovel jobs, handling the cumbersome 3cwt capacity wheelbarrows and large No 10 shovels alongside his Dad and elder brother.

The work was hard, the hours long and the conditions Spartan, yet Jim Monk looks back nostalgically to his formative years in 'a real man's job' on the commercial waterways. Some jobs required a very early start and occasionally Mr J. Monk Snr. woke the boys about 3.30am; as they dressed their Dad prepared breakfast, to be eaten as the lads put on their outdoor clothes and clogs, the preferred wear for Lancashire working folk - a good pair were invaluable, cherished for protecting the feet as well as for their warmth and comfort -meanwhile Mr Monk hurried to the stables on the canal bank about 600 yards from the mooring to get the horse. At Redhouse Bridge (No 68) just south of the village, they met their father leading the horse over the bridge carrying the swingletree, on his shoulder. At the moorings one of the boys cast off the lines, pushed the boat's bows off into the middle of the canal, and threw the five pound hauling line onto the bank, so that their Dad could pick it up and 'hook the horse on;' the other lad went down into the (back) cabin to light a fire in the stove and put the kettle on to boil. The small, square oil lamp that stood on the hatch cover of the fore-cabin was shaded, so as to only show enough light to warn oncoming boats, but whilst a moonlit sky or early dawn light would once have been welcome, in the black-out conditions of World War II the lunar rays presaged the wailing of sirens synonymous with the rising of the dreaded 'bombers moon.' The Tomlinson boats, *George* and *Susie,* were worked in turn, and Jim Monk treasures memories of times when, after walking the horse a bridge length their Dad would climb aboard to take over the steering. As the brothers sheltered in the cabin near to the hatch out of the cold, their Dad told them stories of his own early days working on the L&L as a young lad to help support the family, becoming captain of a boat when he was only in his early teens. Owing to these circumstances the young Jim Monk never had any formal schooling, and it is a tribute to his strength of character and acumen that he went on to build up a fleet which was to bear a respected name in the annals of inland waterway carriers. The period of which Mr J. Monk Snr. spoke was one when the Aberdeen Colliery Tip near the Monk's home was open and the youthful captain used to load there, working the Wigan Coal & Iron Company's boats. This firm had one of the largest boatyards on the canal, with three 'side slips' down which new boats were launched broadside on, and at their peak owned about seventy boats. Their yard was located near the top of Wigan Locks where the old Haigh Ironworks used to be (and where parts of the Isle of Man's famous *Lady Isabella* water wheel at Laxey were built).

The boys were also regaled with stories of long, bitter winters when the ice-boats were out day after day trying to keep the canal open, the maintenance men standing on the deck of the 'breaker' with its specially strengthened bows, either side of a stout rope lashed round the three masts, their breath condensing in the bitter cold, and the horses made to gallop furiously on the dangerously slippery bank, whilst the ice breaker was rocked from side to side by the men on board. Ice breaking was very hard on the animals, (hired for about six shillings a day from the men who were otherwise laid off), because the horses were constantly being brought up short in their collars as the boat hit solid ice, this could cause damage to the shoulders, a condition known as 'slipping' and whilst a horse might continue working it would never really recover, their 'wind' might also be affected together with the ever present danger of the animals (and the men running with them) finishing up 'in the cut', and Mr Monk would only loan his horses in exceptional circumstances. Some of the men sharpened the horses' shoes by filing them, but although this gave a better grip on the ice, the down-side was that the animal could inflict a nasty injury on itself if it stumbled or fell; a temporary expedient was to pack the hoof and shoe with axle-grease, but as soon as the snow 'balled up' beneath the hoof 'clods' of snow and soil fell off as the horse ran and the grease came away also.

Mr J Monk Snr and his two sons concentrated on doing contract work, carrying bulk loads in preference to handling general merchandise, with its attendant problems of storage and warehousing, insurance and the chores of general administration.

Leeds & Liverpool Canal. Maghull. Proceeding northwards from Liverpool, beyond Aintree, its racecourse, and the village of Melling is Maghull, and a sequence of swing bridges. That in our 'period' photograph is being negotiated by a horse-drawn 'short-boat', claiming right of way over one against the opposite bank. Note the decorated square stern, with button fenders, and swan's neck, side rails, a tin bath, in which buckets are stored, the water keg and 'pigeon box' ventilator. The steerswoman wears the customary white apron; a male figure stands on the bridge behind her. The left-hand one of the two forward towing posts is observed, but the line from the horse is fixed to the third mast or lutchet, which could be positioned according to the height of the cargo which is securely sheeted. ***J.Peden***

The large firms such as the Canal Carrying Co., owned not only the boats but the horses as well, so their men had little say in the choice of which horse they had, taking whatever the stableman gave them, but in the case of No.1's like Mr Monk, whilst the wooden boats were usually company owned the provision of a horse and its care, housing and fodder, was part of the captain's contract with the boat owner. There was no preferred breed of boat horse, but the ideal would be a medium sized beast of about 14 hands in height, a quiet tractable animal, that could be trained in the skipper's particular way of working. Word soon travelled along the towpath 'grapevine' if anyone was thinking of selling, or buying a horse and farmers would sometimes display a horse which they had on offer, putting it to graze in their field beside the canal. Someone who had only one or two boats, or perhaps had an animal lame or sick, could usually hire a spare horse from a carrier or farmer who was not too busy, this usually proved to be cheaper than renting an animal from a dealer.

The working life of a horse was between ten and fifteen years and it made good sense to treat the animals well, because if one went sick and became unable to work the boat was laid off, and there were no wages. So the 'good' skippers and horse marines were always alert to any signs of lameness or stumbling and attended to the horse before having their own food, examining the hooves and removing stones, rubbing the animal down and making sure that there were no sore places where the collar or harness had chafed. If problems arose, there were traditional remedies; a palliative for shoulder blisters was to bathe the area with brine; pitch thinned with turps was used to relieve harness sores, and the mouth needed regular inspection to guard against the formation of gumboils, which if discovered would be excised by some device such as a sharp nail first sterilised in boiling water.

The harness was comparatively straightforward, 'hames' were fastened to the collar and side ropes went to the 'swingletree' which rested just below the horse's hind-quarters; the tow-line was attached to this 'swingletree.' On the Leeds & Liverpool canal the side ropes were threaded through leather tubes to prevent them from chafing the horse's flanks, rather than through the gaudily painted bobbins which performed the same function for a narrow-boat harness; webbing across the back kept the swingletree up on its side-ropes and the towing line was attached to the centre of the swingletree and then to the 'lutchet' on the boat, although according to conditions, say when working against a cross wind or in and out of a basin, the rope might be taken round a bollard anywhere on the boat according to where the 'pull' was required. There were many differing methods that the horse-marines used to get a loaded boat moving without putting too much strain on the horse, from the use of pulleys and double-purchases, to guiding the rope round vertical rollers, permanently fitted by the canal proprietors on the inner side of a towpath at an awkward bridge or sharp bend to prevent lines binding and fraying.

A relative who was a retired boatman owned the two stall, wooden stable beside the canal where the 'Monk' horse was kept. Feed was bought in lots of one cwt of oats, one cwt of bran and an enormous bag of chopped hay. The mix comprised 'chop' and a pailful each of oats and bran, mixed together in sufficient quantity to fill three, one cwt sacks at a time. They were stored in the fore cabin together with a full bale of hay which was fed from a net hung round the horse's neck, whilst provender was given in a nose-tin or bucket, usually when going through locks. Despite the early start it might be eight or nine o'clock at night before they got the horse back to the stables, next to which was a small cabin where the elderly owner spent most of his time. During the winter months he kept a roaring fire going in the old boat stove he had fixed up in his private lair, and dried out the boy's wet top coats ready for them to wear the next morning. He was 'good' with horses and kept a pan of water boiling on the stove. When the beast was walked over the canal bridge into the stable, the old man washed out the 'proven' bucket, and made the animal a drink by mixing the contents of a two tin lb of black treacle in boiling water, given to the horse when still hot but off

Leeds & Liverpool Canal. Wigan. Albert Blundell 'walks' the horse drawing one of his Dad's, boats towards Wigan Top Lock. This scene of six decades ago indicates how bleak the outskirts of some colliery towns were. The normal crew was two men and the steerer probably Finch Blundell. The communities were so close knit that if 'Finch,' Jim Monk Snr. or indeed any other Skipper needed assistance in unloading, on nearing their destination there would almost certainly be some 'crony' walking or cycling home from the 'mill' along the cut, or just 'passing the time' who could be called upon to help. A shout of "Are you coming up then" as the boat was steered towards the bank, was sufficient invitation for their friend to jump aboard, perhaps handing his bicycle up first. Three men could unload a boat in about 2½ hours, with the Skipper, his mate and the 'odd man' each "emptying a bay" and earning between 8/- to 12/-, (40p to 60p) perhaps justifying a 'quick pint' at the local before going home for a meal.
Albert Blundell Collection

Monton Old Bridge. Two vintage horse-drawn boats enhance this pastoral scene on the Leigh Branch of the Bridgewater Canal, north of Eccles. To the right of the bridge appear the buildings of the L&NWRly's Monton Green Station. It was necessary for this canal bridge to be reconstructed c1900 so that Salford Corporation electric tramcars could work a route to Peel Green, via Parrin Lane, Winton and New Lane. Contractors for the Eccles Council finished the work in 1905 and the first open top, unvestibuled car worked over the single track running over the centre of the new bridge on the 1st June that year. In addition to being noted for its 'Eccles Cakes.' the area around Monton and Walkden is associated with mining history. The Old Worke Dam Brindley's original reservoir is nearby, as is the Old Colliery Basin from which access was gained to the network of underground waterways, which eventually covered 40 miles, serving the Duke of Bridgewater's coal mines. ***John Ryan***

the boil, it prevented or alleviated croup and other equine respiratory ailments. The main cabin of the horse-drawn boats was at the stern; ropes, a spare towing line (they were about 80 feet long and quickly wore out) a spare tiller etc, were kept in the fore-cabin, but when motors were fitted the back cabin was converted into an engine room and the front end became the main cabin/living quarters. Ropes were always spliced, knots being considered dangerous but even so a spliced noose was never used on the towing mast, instead a loop comprising two or three yards of rope was just hung on the pin, half hitches were not used either as it was considered that the effect of another boat passing at speed might be to tighten a hitch to such a degree that it could not be freed, and the rope would then have to be cut so that the submerged length would not get caught up on the oncoming boat's rudder, which could result in the horse being dragged into the canal, whereas the 'looped' rope could easily be shaken free. This particular hazard stemmed from the fact that rudder blades were strengthened by an iron strip fitted to the bottom edge which often become loosened or damaged when a boat, as often happened struck some underwater obstruction and the projecting piece of metal was likely to 'snag' any ropes which came into contact with it, even in those days there was debris and rubbish in the canals. Care was necessary when passing through bridges; the Leeds & Liverpool 'short-boats' were constructed a little over fourteen feet wide so as to just fit the locks, they also only just cleared the bridge-holes, and if a horse which was a 'bit of a runner' approached a bridge too fast the water would rise in front of the bows and the boat would jar to a halt in the 'bridge-hole', when the sudden shock and pull on the tow-line could all too easily drag the horse into the cut.

For an inexperienced horse this could be disastrous as the animal might get into a panic, and in the course of its struggles become entangled in its harness and drown, so if the worst happened the horse-marine had to jump in after his charge to hold up it's head out of the water. This was a risky exercise also, for whilst in the worst possible scenario some horses would panic others would go down without a fight like a stone, in both cases taking the man with them. It was less of a problem if a horse had 'been in before' as at various points along the bank, two foot wide ramps were inset longitudinally into the edge of the towpath so that horses that had fallen into the 'cut' could be led up out of the water.

The masts called Middle and Forward on Monk boats fitted into steel lined 'Shutts' about two inches deep, cut into the hold timbers, and secured by fastening them against the 'beam' with a rope lashing; the term could also apply to the heavy bottom planks lining the hold. The rear quarters in the wooden horse-boats were snug, but headroom was very limited, and the side decks above the bed-holes leaked, unless they were regularly dowsed with buckets of water during dry hot spells of weather to stop them from shrinking. The main feature was an open-fronted stove sitting in an ash-pan, having a fender and clip-on hob for boiling a kettle and preparing Lancashire hot-pot, or frying bacon to slap between two 'door-stops' of bread making the tasty and nourishing Lancashire 'collops' which could be eaten whilst on the move. Fitted benches were built around the sides, with storage holes beneath and two 'bed-holes above'; there were small cupboards, pantries, a few brass ornaments and provender for the horse in a tub or locker topped up as used from the sacks in the fore cabin. Water, which was ladelled out by means of a dipper was kept in a five gallon keg on the foredeck, well tarred on the inside to keep the contents sweet. Yorkshire built boats had stoves of a more ornamental pattern, and distinctive square, steel lined wooden chimneys.

Many of the Leeds and Liverpool canal boats were registered at Liverpool, especially the Canal Transport boats with which Mr J. Monk Senior's friend Ben Walls was associated. However, other boats engaged on the 'coal jobs' were mainly registered at Blackburn, which was the base for the principal Coal Agents such as Dean Waddington, Crook and Thompson, J W Tomlinson and Henry Croasdale etc.

To ascertain whether they complied with regulations the living quarters were examined by an Inspector from the appropriate Health Department, whose main concern was to measure the internal dimensions and then calculate the volume in cubic feet, to ensure that the figure conformed with the minimum amount of air space considered as suitable for the accommodation of three or four occupants. The standard of furnishings e.g. bunks and other fittings, including what the boatmen called a 'Spare Side' also came under scrutiny. Some cabins only contained bunks or 'bed-holes' for 2 people on one side, and the opposite side was designated the 'Spare Side' where another person could sleep on occasion. It was not obligatory for a boat only engaged on day work to be inspected and registered but most boats were certificated in case the need to sleep on board arose.

THE COAL JOB, STEAMERS AND 'WIDDOP' ENGINES

At first, Monk's worked mainly 'on the coal job' for Tomlinson's on that stretch of the Leeds & Liverpool canal between Wigan and Blackburn. Regular deliveries were made to the Talbot Mill at Chorley, the Pioneer Mill at Mill Hill, and Hall Street Mill above Sam's Lock the second in the Blackburn flight.

At the Talbot Mill the loaded barrows were wheeled along 14ft long planks leading to a stage, and the contents tipped into small tub wagons which two men ran down a tramway to the coal stack near the firehole. At other destinations a gangway of planks made a 'walk' along which the heavy barrows were trundled.

Finch Blundell, another boat owner and close friend of the Monk boys and their Dad, who lived first at Botany Bay and then at Chorley, also dealt in boat ropes, hauling lines, and hay and feed for the boat horses. Finch and his son Albert worked on the Talbot Mill job along with Monks' and when his dad died Albert took over the business and employed a local man named Harry Wilcock as his mate.

Contemporary with Tomlinson's other carriers were Dean Waddington's, and Crook & Thompson's, their boats known as the 'Black Diamonds' from the style of decoration, whilst another carrier, Henry Croasdale had a prestigious contract with the Wiggins Teape Paper Mill at Withnall. Every Mill Engineer had a preferred supplier and favourite type of coal, be it nuts, slack or cobs, won from a particular seam which he considered to be the best for steam raising at his own plant. Conversely each merchant had their favoured clientele; Dean Waddington's serviced the Sun and Star Paper Mills at Feniscowles, together with Bains' and other established Cotton Mills in the Blackburn area, in addition to the Whitebirk Power Station.

During World War II the construction of new boats was restricted and this shortage was surmounted by the practice of 'rebuilding' old horse boats. The worn-out boat was scrapped but the keel and bottom planks were retained to form the basis of a

Lydiate. Nine miles from Southport and eleven miles from Liverpool, two well laden horse-drawn boats meander along this lovely stretch of the L&L Canal, the leading horse just out of the frame into the bridge hole. A famous local hostelry, 400 yards from Bridge 17A, is said to date from 1320 and has an inscription above the door to prove it. Built around a dead tree it was originally called The Royal Oak but became The Scotch Piper following the invasion of the Highlanders supporting Bonnie Prince Charlie in 1745, when the landlord's daughter fell in love with a piper wounded during fighting in the area, nursed him back to health and eventually married him. Locally the pub is also known as 'Owd Lollies' - the aforementioned 'Lollie's Bridge' No 17A perpetuating the memory of a ganger foreman who, during the construction of the canal used it as his unofficial headquarters and partook of substantial libations when facing problems. ***J. Peden***

nominal 'rebuild' that was in all but name a new boat. J & W Tomlinson's horse boat *George* was so treated and emerged from the dry-dock as a motor boat.

The idea of using steamers on the L&L was discussed as far back as 1852 and the merits of internal combustion engines debated 50 years later, but horses continued in use until about 1960; one of the last horse-drawn coal boats was Ainscough's (H & R. Ainscough) *Parbold,* engaged in conveying boiler slack from the colliery tips to the firm's own Mills at Parbold and Burscough.

Steam had however been tried out on the Bridgewater Canal as early as the end of the previous century, when a steam powered stern wheel paddle-tug was built c.1798 and experimentally put to work hauling barges laden with coal; although the speed attained was no greater than that of horse drawn boats it was thought that the wash might damage the banks and the oddly named *Bonaparte* was banished to the Duke's mines at Worsley, where it spent the greater part of the next 100 years working as a stationary engine pumping water from the labyrinthine workings.

Another notable event reputedly took place in 1830, when four small Manchester built iron steamers passed through the Mersey & Irwell Navigation locks on a delivery trip to Liverpool, and towards the end of the decade two iron screw steamers, the *Countess of Ellesmere* and *President*, were at work ferrying passengers along the River Irwell from Manchester to the pleasure grounds at Pomona Gardens, later to be the site of the Manchester Ship Canal Docks.

(Above) Blackburn. Typical loaded horse-boat, seen when "muck was money," "coal was king," and atmospheric pollution a secondary consideration. A small market town in the 1790's, with a cottage industry in hand-loom weaving, by the end of the Victorian era Blackburn would be the greatest cotton weaving town in the world. That industry is now decimated, but artifacts remain. The impressive canal buildings at Enam Wharf now incorporate a pub, business and visitor centre, and there is much to interest the industrial archeologist, the Lewis Textile Museum, with examples of working machinery, a fine Museum and Art Gallery, a church dating from 1820 raised to Cathedral status in 1926, whilst despite modernisation, there is no doubt that this was once the capital of "King Cotton" and there is the flight of six locks, having surmounted which one is 400ft above sea level. ***L.Monk Collection***

(Left) Nr. Marsland Green Colliery, Leigh. Late 1940's. A view from a towed 'dumb boat' of motor *Spica* working hard, with Mr J Monk Snr steering. ***L.Monk Collection***

A "CHRISTMAS CARD" JOURNEY

A WIDDOP DIVERSION

The rebuilt *George* was fitted with a WIDDOP 21hp engine, a British made unit then popular with the boatmen and owners alike. Dean Waddington's for instance, had 'WIDDOP' installed in five of their fleet. The new *George's* engine was not altogether satisfactory, so Mr Monk arranged with Tomlinson's the boat's owner's that he should take the *George* up to Yorkshire for the engine installation to be checked by its makers at Stockbridge.

It was mid-winter when Mr J Monk Snr and his two sons began the long journey from their home at Adlington to Keighley; the Leeds & Liverpool canal was thick with ice and weather conditions for their trans-Pennine expedition were anything but inviting, although the steep hills around Withnell Fold presented a 'Christmas card' aspect. They passed the short northward facing Walton Summit Branch (of the Lancaster Canal) near the Johnson's Hillock flight, and crossed the high embankment which led to Blackburn, but Wilfred became increasingly unwell as they proceeded through the Calder Valley and, after they had passed through the 559 yard long Gannow Tunnel he was taken to Burnley Hospital where, once assured that he was out of danger Wilf was left to recover whilst 17 year old Jim and his dad continued their journey.

The rounded mass of Pendle Hill loomed above Brierfield with its cobbled streets and terraced houses, and they negotiated the seven Barrowford Locks to pass through the 1640 yard long Foulridge Tunnel and by way of Barnoldswick (pronounced 'Barlick') through the lovely countryside around Gargrave, then down the six Bank Newton Locks into the Upper Airedale Valley. On then through the ancient town of Skipton, passing the entrance

(Above) Stretford, Tues. 16 Jan 1962. James Monk & Son's one-time horse-boat *George,* rebuilt and converted to a motor during WW2, the only Monk boat not to have it's name painted on the bow, speeds to Runcorn Gas Works with an urgently required load of boiler slack. The skipper, Mr J Monk Snr, is well wrapped up against the bitter weather, with a sack worn three cornered over his cap for extra protection, and a blazing 'fire-devil' formed from an empty drum precariously balanced on the stern.
H.Arnold. Waterway Images

(Right) Twenty Steps Locks MSC Sat. 19 Mar 1961. Mr J Monk Jnr. is setting the lock under the Northwich Road Swing Bridge, leading to the truncated length of the Runcorn & Latchford Canal, for their *Irwell* and *June,* working from Ellesmere Port bound via the R&L for Manor Lock, the River Mersey and Howley Quay laden with aluminium ingots. ***N.Jones***

to Lord Thanet's Canal (The Springs Branch); the ancient town and its picturesque High Street overlooked by the Norman Castle, with its six great round towers. Then down the Aire valley to Stockbridge, where the town of Keighley stood about a mile distant across the valley.

Young Jim then had to make his own way home across country by bus and train, whilst Mr J Monk Snr. stayed with the boat until WIDDOP's removed the engine for inspection. Wilf was back home by the time *George's* engine was overhauled and the trio set out once more for Stockbridge to collect the *George*. The engineers reported that - amongst other things - the engine had been running cool, and to raise the working temperature they fitted a constricting bobbin in the water line to reduce the flow, added a 12 inch thermometer so that the boatmen could monitor the engine's working temperature, and altered the layout from the standard WIDDOP 'wet' exhaust to a 'dry' system, with the water discharging through a separate branch.

There was no doubt that the modification worked; Mr Monk recalls conditions in the engine house as being 'mad hot' with the new thermometer stuck on its top mark as they came through Withnall, passing Wiggins Teape's Mill at about 7 o'clock at night. Although Monk's, especially Wilf later became skilled in fitting and tuning boat engines, when motor boats first began to oust horse-boats the fitters at Mayor's Wigan Boatyard (1932-1959), were the acknowledged experts, the Tarleton based concern had taken over the Canal Company's Wigan Boatyard and fitting shop. So off the Monks' went next morning with the overheating *George* to the Wigan yard. A fitter examined the installation and said 'I'll have a ride over 'The Moss' with you', (the stretch of open land below Poolstock Locks) towards P & K's tip 'and see how it shapes up!' Mayor's man stood on the bottom step of the engine house ladder and as the WIDDOP thumped along towards the tip the engine temperature rose spectacularly and the thermometer went off the scale. Suddenly to everyone's amusement the mechanic ran up on deck shouting, 'Come on let me off this engine's going to blow up.' However no disaster followed and as Mr Monk said, they had 'brought it all the way from Yorkshire like that'. The problem was solved by reaming out the bobbin to allow a greater flow of water through the cooling system and the modifications improved the engine's performance so much that other WIDDOP fitted boats were similarly modified, and the dry exhaust became a standard feature.

In horse boat days sometimes the tips were closed when Monks arrived on their last trip of the day and in that case the boat was moored alongside the tip overnight whilst the crew would walk home to Adlington along the canal bank, taking turns to ride on the horse reversing the procedure on their return the following morning.

When the horse-boats were supplanted by diesels a new work plan was adopted; when they had loaded at the tip the previous night), *George* was brought back to their overnight mooring close to home at Red House Bridge so that they could leave for the Talbot Mill at about 5.30am. Arriving at Chorley the trio emptied the boat with spade and barrow, each taking a bay. Returning

Astley. Jan 1956. Albert Blundell's *Christine* and *Finch* passing through Astley on the Leigh Branch of the Bridgewater Canal laden with coal for the Power Stations. ***Leonard Monk Collection***

The Wigan Flight. c.1950. Dean Waddington's *Elsie* ascending. Skipper Ernie Parkinson is beside the balance beam on the right, and Mate Eddie Lee is on the left. ***Leonard Monk Collection***

Nr. Adlington Gas Works. c.1949. A coal laden *George* moored in a delightfully rural setting despite it's proximity to industry. ***Leonard Monk Collection***

"HOLD IN - HOLD OUT"

Empty boats going down from Blackburn to Wigan and beyond took the right-hand, e.g. tow-path side when passing oncoming traffic but on the Bridgewater Canal, once Leigh Basin was reached, left-hand 'Rule of the Road' applied. On the L & L it was all too easy to accidentally put an empty boat on the bank, so the horse-tenter, when meeting a loaded boat would shout 'Hold in' to his mate at the tiller instructing him to direct the bow towards the bank; before it touched he would call 'Hold out' and, as the boat then straightened up parallel to the bank jump on to the towpath, run to the horse pulling the oncoming (loaded) boat and push the animal's head towards the hedge, to stop it from pulling, this caused the tow-line to slacken and sink so that the empty boat could pass over it safely; the line might otherwise foul the empty boat's rudder and drag the horse backwards into the canal as recounted earlier.

Another 'dodge' was to detach the line from the horse, coil it and then - of course retaining the end - throw the coil into the 'cut', when its weight and mass ensured that it sank, rather than floated. When both boats had passed safely the line could be hooked back onto the horse which could be released to 'walk-on' and immediately it felt the rope tighten, would put it's head down in the collar

Aspull Top Lock (No.65)Wigan Flight, January 1956. The gates are set for a loaded Blackburn bound Dean Waddington boat. The Wigan Coal & Iron Co's Aspull Boatyard was adjacent to the lock in it's day, but modern housing estates and developments have vastly altered Wigan's skyline and 'flat cap' image. This flight of 21 wide and deep locks raising the canal by about 200ft, start just beyond the point where the Leigh Branch leaves the main line to join up with the Bridgewater Canal. At a 'T' Junction beyond Top Lock the L & L joins what was the southern end of the Lancaster Canal, and continues along what the working boatmen knew as 'The Lancaster Pool', a 9 mile lock free pound, the early stages affording a panoramic vista of the country below before the canal entered the woodlands of Haigh Park and Hall. ***L Monk Collection***

Red House Bridge, Adlington. October 1947. A Dean Waddington 'motor' stranded on a de-watered section of the Leeds & Liverpool Canal at Red House Bridge, this was a favourite mooring point for boatmen living locally, and is also the Bridge *(Page 14)* over which Mr J.Monk Snr used to lead the horse from their stable, in the early morning to join his young sons who were preparing the boat, moored near the bridge for an early start. The small town of Adlington then housed a canal based community, with most folk as at home on the boats as the land. The next bridge was No 69 White Bear Bridge, now the site of a Marina *(Page 22)*. The 305ft contour line is reached here and the heights of Winter Hill (1,488ft), Smithills Moor and Rivington Peak 1,190ft with its tower, look down on the Rivington Lower and Anglezarke Reservoirs and across the valley to the line of the Leeds & Liverpool Canal, proceeding to the market town of Chorley on the west bank.
L Monk Collection

and proceed on its steady plod without needing any further prompting. One lock at Johnson's Hillock had a very short pound, called 'The Crooked Pool', where it was impossible for empty and loaded boats to pass unless the boat 'going down' was pulled out of the empty lock into the hollow (or crook) of the pool whilst the loaded boat passed. When that boat was clear, the rope of the empty boat was 'hooked on' and the horse sent off at a gallop, this swung the bow out of the hollow and into the middle of the pool when the steerer would shout 'Pull in', on which the horse-tenter reeled the line in short, just as the boat was entering the lock entrance, so stopping the boat from crashing into and rebounding off the walls. Jim Monk recalled that it only took about six or seven seconds to execute the whole seemingly complex manoeuvre which was done, 'almost without thinking.'

A vital part of the horse-boatman's equipment was a home-made whip, primarily used for giving audible signals to other water-borne traffic. A round handle, often taken or carved from a suitable branch was fitted with a leather thong, to which was secured a length of braided grass string, or an animal tail for a lash. The sound was produced by holding the whip vertically, then swinging it smartly round the head, and pulling it back sharply to produce a loud crack like a gun-shot when approaching bridges or other blind spots. The first of two boats travelling in conflicting directions to 'crack' took the right of way. The sound also warned the skippers of motor boats who 'knocked down' their engines when approaching bridge-holes so that they could hear any horse-boatman 'cracking'.

The change from horse-drawn to motor boats continued, but trade slackened as World War II neared its end and large firms, like Canal Transport Ltd., (whose shareholders were the former Lancashire Canal Transport Co, the Liverpool Warehousing Co Ltd and the Leeds & Liverpool Canal Co.) hired out some of their older boats to the smaller carriers. Mr J. Monk Snr. moved his operations to the Bridgewater Canal where trade remained brisk, and hired Canal Transport boats, as did Dean Waddington's and other carriers.

NATIONALISATION - FOCUS ON MANCHESTER

It was not long after the 1st January 1948 when the Leeds & Liverpool Canal, and much of the country's inland waterway network came under the control of the British Transport Commission's Docks & Inland Waterways Executive, that Mr. J. Monk Snr. took on contract work for the Stretford Corporation, delivering coal to the Power Stations, a destination which entailed leaving the main line of the L & L and joining its Leigh Arm,

Skipton L & L Canal. ND. *Florence* owned by J.R.Thornton of Skipton approaching Gallows Bridge, Mr David Lowe, learnt from former canal foreman Mr Harry Binns that *Florence* was possibly built by Riders at Leeds, her Captain is probably Bill Hesketh and the mate Freddie Barrett, who was Mr Thornton.'s son-in-law. Steam engines, introduced in 1875 were used until the mid-fifties, the last being *Thomas* built for W. Holden of Skipton in 1936 by Harker's of Knottingley. Mr Holden also bought ex L & L Steamer No 41, which he had converted to diesel. ***H Arnold - Waterway Images***

which made an end on junction with the Bridgewater Canal. A trip of some eight miles through Marsland Green, Astley Green, Worsley and Eccles, brought into view the imposing structure of the Barton Swing Aqueduct, which carries the Bridgewater Canal across the Manchester Ship Canal. Here, the horses, still towing, were led up a ramp and along a narrow platform attached to the side girders of the aqueduct, although should a 'mate' with a motor boat be about to cross also, a tow was sure to be offered, which meant that the horse could be unhooked and 'walked' over. It was then only a short distance to the Barton Power Station which lay on the west side of the Bridgewater Canal (opposite to an oil depot) and between the aqueduct and Ashburton Road Bridge.

Boats making deliveries to the Stretford Power Station continued to Waters Meeting, where they 'turned left' onto the main line of the Bridgewater Canal, and proceeded towards the Trafford Park Estate, and Pomona Docks, the power station being situated on the north bank opposite to the Manchester United Football Ground on the south side. It was soon evident that the transfer of activities to the Bridgewater Canal had been a wise move and whilst their Dad got a grip on the Manchester traffic, Jim and Wilfred Monk continued running Tomlinson's *George* on the L & L.

Wilf then moved away to help his father with the Bridgewater Canal work but Jim continued working the *George*, assisted by his mate Dick Davies until the time when Jim, too joined his Dad and brother on the Bridgewater and Manchester Ship Canal traffic.

As the Monk fleet expanded and more boats were acquired additional crew members were needed, but there was no shortage of skilled watermen around Adlington; most of their neighbours worked on Monk boats occasionally, but some, notably Ernie Parkinson, Bill Crank, Tommy Cullen, Hughie Martland, Bill Mayo, and John Mailley, were regular employees.

Ample work became available for the 'carriers by water' who had moved away from their roots on the Leeds & Liverpool Canal, for following the end of World War II the MSC had made an extensive investment in modernising and improving their dock system. As his share of the Bridgewater and Manchester Docks traffic increased, in step with the volume of trade passing through the Port of Manchester, Mr J. Monk Snr found it necessary to increase his fleet and more boats were at first hired and then purchased from Canal Transport Ltd, whilst from J & W Tomlinson's came their *George*, which on Mr Monk's recommendation had already been

Stretford Power Station. Bridgewater Canal. c.1950. Albert Bendell's dumb boat *Irene* is being lightened at the suction discharge plant; the men move the suction pipe ends around the hold, manoeuvring them as required to clear the coal by means of the moveable overhead booms. Monk's *George* lying ahead of the *Irene* will be discharged next, whilst two of the T&W Wells' empty boats are moving away from the plant in this atmospheric setting characteristic of the period. The power station *(left)* was demolished some years ago, and the coal stockyard *(right)* aquired by Manchester United FC. ***Boat Museum Trust***

Poolstock Gardens, Wigan. c.1948/9. The Leigh Branch of the Leeds & Liverpool Canal left the main line between Wigan Power Station and the 22nd lock. In 1900 a burst led to the Ince Hall Colliery branch being infilled and subsidence on Ince Moss and the Leigh Branch led to the construction of the two Poolstock Locks, which needed rebuilding in 1913 after further canal subsidence. James Monk's *Spica,* later named *Wilfred,* is seen at Poolstock shortly after the end of World War 11. ***L.Monk Collection***

fitted with a Thornycroft marine type engine, replacing the WIDDOP installation which had been the subject of the arduous winter expedition to Keighley, and the subsequent experiments with the 'dry' exhaust system.

Monks' no longer needed to call on the services of outside fitters, and installed themselves a 4 cylinder 40 hp Russell Newbery engine in the *Wilfred*, originally called *Spica*, and a three cylinder 30 hp Russell Newbery engine in the *Marion*; *Irwell* was also fitted with an engine of this marque, but *Jean* was powered by a superb four cylinder Thornycroft marine type engine, said to be similar to those in the Cunard lifeboats, rigorously serviced during 'turn-round' between voyages by their makers. Jim was friendly with a Thornycroft engineer who said that their fitters remained aboard the great liners, working until satisfied that the engines were in A1 condition, even going offshore and returning with the pilot boat or possibly making the round trip 'out and back' if that was necessary.

To Mr J. Monk Snr. and his two sons -and indeed, most folk the 1950's seemed promising as wartime austerities were relaxed and the country got back towards normality. Many of the ships now visiting Manchester's busy Docks were former Liberty and Victory class vessels purchased as replacements for tonnage lost to U boat attack. There were far more classes than is generally realised, the principal Liberty type was EC2-S-C1 and Victory types included VC2-S-AP2; VC2-S-AP3 etc., in any case, they were now garbed in peace-time liveries, their gun housings and quick release life-rafts superfluous but many of them went on to render sterling service, often under foreign flags for many years. These vessels were gradually replaced by a new generation of smart new British built cargo liners (the day of the container vessel and ugly 'box' boats had not yet come!) naval architects still in the main, adhering to tradition designed what would be the last generation of 'break-bulk' type cargo liners for general trade, having sea-kindly lines, graceful sheer, recognisable funnels and pleasing superstructures.

Johnson's Hillock Locks. Whittle, Nr. Chorley. 1950's. Leaving the gates set Jim Monk and *Jean* depart for the Star Paper Mills, Blackburn or Whitebirk Power Station. Beyond the flight the canal runs north east towards Withnell Fold and Riley Green. A canal cottage marked the junction with the old Walton Summit Branch, and an old toll house stood close to the middle lock. Following negotiations in the 1860's the North End of the Lancaster Canal was leased to the London & North Western Railway, whilst the South End between Walton Summit and Wigan Top Lock, including Johnson's Hillock Locks were leased to the Leeds & Liverpool Canal in perpetuity for £7,075 pa from 1 August 1864.
L Monk Collection

Johnson's Hillock Locks. Whittle, Nr. Chorley. 1950's. *Jean* Reg No 16 at Liverpool, newly lettered, engine throttled right down, is moving very slowly out of the lock, and Jim Monk will step aboard after securing the paddle-gear, as Jean draws level with him. Work on the construction of the Yorkshire-Lancashire waterway began after its Act was passed in 1770 and the lock-free section from Bingley to Skipton was opened by 1777, but finance was difficult and the main line from Leeds to Liverpool was not opened until 1816, following an arrangement to share a ten mile length of the Lancaster Canal, from Wigan Top Lock to Johnson's Hill Bottom Lock. The length of the Lancaster towards Preston became the Walton Summit Branch.
L Monk Collection

In January 1954 when the new Queen Elizabeth II Dock adjacent to the entrance locks at Eastham was opened by the MSC especially to accommodate tankers of 30,000 tons deadweight, the Manchester dock estate, visited annually by over 4,000 cargo vessels covered an area of 700 acres, comprising 179 acres of water space and $5^{1}/_{2}$ miles of quays, supported by a port railway system having a track length of more than 200 miles served by 75 locomotives and 2,900 wagons.

At this time there were over 200 factories on the bustling Trafford Park industrial estate, employing between them some 50,000 workers, whilst Manchester was the third most important port in the British Isles, the traffic handled there annually exceeding 12 million tons, as compared with the 925,000 tons that arrived at the Port of Manchester in its opening year.

BLOOM STREET POWER STATION & THE ROCHDALE NINE FLIGHT OF LOCKS

A 'coal job' very much Monk's "own" since their 'horse-boat days took them down the Leigh Branch to Waters Meeting at Stretford, where they then turned left and carried on through Trafford Park, passing Hulme Locks to Castlefield Junction to join the Rochdale Canal, and work part-way up the 'Rochdale Nine flight' into Manchester's city centre, laden with coal for the Bloom Street Power Station, opened in 1901, primarily to provide power for the city's street lights and tram-cars, the adjacent City of Manchester's, Dickinson Street Electric Light Station, also a coal fired power plant and the city's first, opened by the Lord Mayor, Alderman Anthony Marshall JP on 31 July 1893 having insufficient capacity to cope with the growing demand.

Bickershaw Colliery, Plank Lane, Leigh. c.1950. Some household coal was handled by merchants and contractors, like Crook and Thompson Ltd, T W Wells, and Dean Waddington's, but by the 1920/30's most coal traffic was delivered to the textile mills, conveniently situated on the canal's bank; as they changed to electric power, supplied first by local generating stations, then the national grid, the carriers won contracts for supplying coal to the power stations. Bickershaw Colliery lay on the Leigh arm of the L&L marked by a swing bridge, (now a mechanically worked lift bridge.) Beyond the next bridge, 'Springfield' and in Leigh proper, 10 miles 6 furlongs from Stretford-Waters Meeting, the 'Leeds' makes an end on junction with the Bridgewater Canal, although there is no stop-lock to indicate this. Dean Waddington's *Roger,* seen right, is in the foreground of boats, either loaded or waiting to load for the Wigan Power Station. Dean Waddington's, Crook & Thompson and Henry Croasdale were taken over by Hargreaves (Leeds) Ltd in the 1950's.
L Monk Collectionn

Garswood Hall Tip, c.1950. Skipper Jack Prendergast, in charge of Dean Waddington's *Peter,* (which has the mast set for going up the flight) seen hauling on a line, with one foot on the bank and the other on the boat is manouvering *Peter* into position beneath the end-opening wooden-bodied coal wagon on the tippler (top.) When the boat is in position, the operator on the gantry will release the mechanism, the hinged centre portion of the gantry carrying the wagon will rotate to an angle of forty-five degrees and the coal will be discharged through the end door into *Peter's* hold. The tip was gravity worked and the loaded wagons, collected from the colliery by a small steam locomotive were shunted to the top of a gradient and then released to the tippler one at a time. In the early years of WWII four runaway wagons leapt right off the tippler and sank T&W Wells' steamer *Thomas*. Towards the end of the war years Mayor's Boatyard at Wigan built *Peter* which was fitted with a Gardner 2LW engine. ***L Monk Collection***

The Rochdale Canal was opened throughout in 1804. The maximum dimensions of the Rochdale Flats were 72ft x 14ft 2in x 4ft draught, 8ft 11in headroom, 70 tons capacity, Yorkshire Keels 57ft in length and 70ft narrowboats also carried traffic on the waterway.

Excluded from the waterways nationalisation programme The Rochdale Canal was abandoned in 1952, small wonder that Jim Monk Snr. and his sons found progress up the flight of locks to Bloom Street increasingly difficult as time progressed. In the event the 'Bloom Street job' was 'run down' when under the British Electricity Authority's control the coal fed boilers were replaced by an oil fired installation in 1953, although May 1958 has been stated as the date on which the last working boat travelled down to Castlefield from Bloom Street. The Rochdale Canal locks are numbered in sequence from its junction with the Calder & Hebble navigation at Sowerby Bridge; the terminal flight at Manchester comprising Lock Nos 84 - 92, and the Monk boats therefore entered the system at Lock No 92, Dukes, prior to encountering those at Albion Mills, Tib St and Oxford Road, (or Oxford Street, either designation seems to have been used). St Mary's Hospital which came to rely upon 'Bloom Street' for its combined heat and power supplies stood on the right hand bank - on that length the towpath side - of the Rochdale Canal which then passed beneath the busy thoroughfare of Oxford Street. The lock was situated here with the side of St James's Hall, parallel on the left, whilst opposite on the right of the Oxford Street lock was the side of the Palace Theatre. Then on the left-hand side and just beyond the top gates towered the buildings of the Dickinson Street Electric Light Station. Dickinson Street which crossed Portland Street; ended at the Electric Light Station. Separating the Electric Light Station from the Bloom Street Power Station was an arm off the Rochdale canal and where, end on to the Electric Light Station was the impressive red-brick building of the Bloom Street Power

Barton MSC Swing Aqueduct. c1900. This probably posed end on view (the tank was not usually swung loaded) was taken from Bridgewater Canal level, and shows the 1,400 ton 'tank' complete with barge, boatmen, horse and tenter holding its head, on the 'side-towpath' on its gallery 9ft above the water level. A proposal to build two sets of locks to enable 'Bridgewater' traffic to cross the MSC was abandoned in favour of this swing aqueduct. ***J.Peden***

Barton Aqueduct and Road Swing Bridge. c1948. *MSC Arrow,* photo taken from the 'stern' tug *MSC Nymph* both running 'light' to Eastham, from Manchester Docks. Note 'seals' to aqueduct, the pier mainly built of cement concrete with brickwork and granite in the part taking the weight, and the signal mast by the bridgemaster's cabin. "2 Balls Up" denotes Eastham bound traffic. This class of single screw steam tug by Henry Robb Ltd, comprised four powerful 144 gt vessels, with 750 hp two-cylinder compound engines by Aitchison, Blair Ltd. *MSC Arrow* always recognisable by her massive funnel came out in 1938, as did *Archer; Bison* and *Badger* followed in 1939. *MSC Nymph* a 131gt twin screw 770 bhp motor tug also from Robb's of Leith was built in 1942, the last of a class of four *MSC Mallard* and *MSC Merlin* of 1940, and the third *MSC Neptune* of 1941. All names were now prefixed by MSC. ***J.Ashton***

Station, the street from which it was named having crossed Princess Street to end at the edge of the basin. The boiler houses of both the Dickinson Street and Bloom Street stations were parallel to the canal. As constructed Dickinson Street had six coal fired boilers of Galloway design, and a travelling electric crane by Mather & Platt for the purpose of unloading canal barges, Bloom Street had eleven Babcock & Wilcox boilers and two travelling electric cranes for unloading the washed slack similarly, although Jim Monk's recollections are of a Priestman self-propelled steam crane being engaged on this task when their boats were supplying the power station. Looking forward, beneath the Princess Street bridge could be seen the gates of another set of locks where the towpath changed sides and the pavement of Canal Street on the opposite bank was shared by pedestrians and the horses pulling the barges. For ease of location these two power stations can be considered as centrally located in an area bounded by Oxford Street, with Portland Street on the left Princess Street, ahead, crossing the canal - which continued climbing towards its junction with the Ashton Canal - and bounded on the right by Whitworth Street. By the mid 1920's the Dickinson Street plant was more or less a sub-station converting high voltage current to AC, and a joint staff operated the Dickinson Street and Bloom Street plants. the chimney was demolished in 1934, later the old power station office building was demolished, and at the beginning of 1960 the site of Manchester's first power station was occupied by the Linley House building of the North Western Electricity Board (NORWEB). Although the Bloom Street Power Station ceased to produce electricity in 1950, the vital steam heating service to some public buildings and important institutions was maintained and in 1983 customers included The Palace Theatre, Refuge Building and Ritz Ballroom. However in 1984/5 Associated Heat Services took over the Bloom Street CHP installation and the steam traditionally conveyed by large (usually warm to the touch pipes) continued to flow through the system laid along the line of the Rochdale Canal until the service was discontinued in 1989. A length of the pipe, exemplifying this early CHP (combined heat and power) scheme is now preserved at the Museum of Science & Industry in Manchester. Where the heating pipes ran beneath the canal over-bridges it was both warm and dry, and Jim Monk recalls that, especially in the winter-time there were always homeless people or 'tramps' sleeping 'under the arches' and taking refuge from the inclement conditions although the electricity conduits were notoriously frequented by rats and the Bloom Street Power station at least had quite a famous rat-catcher on its staff.

A section of the Rochdale canal (from Castlefield Junction with the Bridgewater Canal to Ducie Street Junction with the Ashton Canal), is accessible to boats 'doing the Cheshire ring' and on 3 May 1996 the Mayor of Calderdale performed the opening ceremony at Sowerby Bridge of the magnificent tunnel, lock and channel, reconnecting the Rochdale Canal to the national waterway network. Canal Society members hope that the waterway will be restored throughout in the early years of this new century.

A 'Bloom Street' delivery was often a 'rush job' for the Monks' with their boat being 'shouted up' at the tips to load 'out of

Stockton Heath. Runcorn & Latchford Canal. Saturday 19 March 1961. Having assisted Mr J Monk Jnr to work their 62ft iron short-boat *Irwell* and also Monk's *June* of which he had charge, through Twenty Steps Lock, dimensions 85ft x 19ft 6in, Tommy Cullen tops up *Irwell's* fuel tank ready for their transit of the canal. Both boats carried Aluminium Ingots, transhipped at Ellesmere Port and destined for the British Alumimum Company at Warrington, via the River Mersey's Howley Quay Wharf and Depot. The environmental impact of the non-degradeable foam, produced by the first generation of detergent based washing powders was becoming apparent, the lock chamber was full and *Irwell's* hull is seen to be coated with clinging masses of the stuff. The Bridgewater Canal opened to Runcorn in 1776, whilst the Runcorn & Latchford Canal was commenced in 1799 and opened in 1804. The course of the R & L beyond Stockton Heath to Runcorn was severed by the new Manchester Ship Canal, leaving just the short section, Twenty Steps Lock on the MSC to Manor (former Latchford) Locks on the River Mersey. ***N.Jones***

turn' as bunker space was limited at 'Bloom Street', and the small reserve stocks held dwindled rapidly when demand was heavy.

Jim Monk recalls that both the canal, and the locks were neglected, silted, and obstructed by rubbish. The gates not only leaked badly but were very heavy and stiff to work, and rubbish that continually accumulated in the locks was dumped by tenants of the terraced houses in the maze of small streets off the city's main thoroughfares. Low water levels were also a constant problem and water might require to be run down from the upper pounds to fill the locks. A welcome helper was Bill Quinne, a retired lockman former long serving Rochdale Canal employee and friend of Jim's. Bill lived nearby and walked down the flight to meet the boats coming up, usually having the first lock set ready for them, and if the boat was single manned working it through for the skipper as he hurried forward to wrestle with the next set of stubborn gates. One of the Monk fleet often used on this coal delivery job was the *Pauline* (I) a dumb boat purchased from Messrs Crook & Thompson of Blackburn, usually worked by Jim's cousin Bill Crank, and towed by whichever motor boat was available, skippered by Mr J Monk Snr, *Pauline* met an untimely end when, whilst unloading her one day at Bloom Street, the crane driver misjudged his angle of lift and allowed the ascending grab to become caught beneath the front edge of a massive stone window sill, which becoming dislodged crashed down onto the *Pauline*, smashing the bottom boards and sinking her. Fortunately no-one was injured, but when salvaged the boat was found to be damaged beyond economic repair.

Trafford Park. Sat. 25 Aug 1956. King Canute granted Ralph Trafford land for military help and land, from William the Conqueror included Stretford, which in the 1890's was a 1,200 acre estate of farms, lake and parklands, centred around Trafford Hall, Sir Humphrey de Trafford, the younger, sold the estate (in 1896) to a developer Mr E.T. Hooley, for what we would call a 'Theme Park' today but Mr Marshall Stevens the M S C General Manager persuaded Mr Hooley, to promote the park as an industrial estate. Mr Stevens left the M S C. to become Managing Director of Trafford Park Estates Ltd, a company launched on 17 August 1896. In 1996 the Trafford Park Development Corporation celebrated the Centenary of the Estate with events like Dragon Boat Races and a Boat Rally, on the waters of the Ontario Basin, formerly one of Manchester's Docks. Wharfside is a key regeneration area, complementing Salford Quays, and with developments at Exchange Quay, Pomona and City Park brings increased status and business to the Trafford Park Urban Development area. The former railway swing bridge on Trafford Wharf Road has been re-located as an amenity feature and provides access for pedestrians from residential properties on one side of the old No 9 Dock to the commercial developments of 'Harbour City' on the other. Four decades earlier Hudswell Clarke & Co, 0-6-0T MSC *No 35 Stockholm Works* No 701 of 1904, passes with a train of heavy steel girders. Far left awaits the author's 1934 Morris 10-4 saloon. ***Norman Jones***

Barton Power Station. Late 1940's. A decidedly atmospheric view of canal traffic in the days of 'King Coal' with laden L&L short-boats, and (centre) with its distinctive stern rails a horse-drawn boat, all assembled in the Barton Arm of the Bridgewater Canal awaiting their turn to unload.
L Monk Collection

"GATHERING COAL FROM THE SEA-SHORE"

However another mishap which happened one morning ,when brother Wilf was working the boat then called *Spica* (later 'enamed *Wilfred*), at the same location ended in tragedy, and the leath of a power station workman who was killed whilst standing n *Spica's* hold assisting with the unloading. The grab descended, ;cooped up about a ton of slack and ascended unusually slowly,)ut when it reached the top of its hoist - at a height of about eighty 'eet - the bucket failed to hook onto the 'nest' of the crane, and lropped back with appalling speed into the bottom of the boat, :rushing a young man working in the hold and smashing the bottom)lanks of the boat which, to add to the tragedy immediately began o sink. During the course of the afternoon Jim Monk heard of the accident whilst passing through Wigan Top Lock, from a boatman vho had heard the news on the radio; although Wilf was not njured all the boatmen were very sad to hear of this young man's intimely death and Wilf attended the inquest at which the verdict vas one of 'accidental death'.

Towards the end of the 'coal burning' era, although the main lemand for water-borne fuel supplies was at the Barton and Trafford Park Power Stations, some trips entailed a right turn at Waters Meeting onto the Bridgewater Canal, with deliveries for he Linotype printing works at Sale, and Monk boats often :ontinued on through Heatley, Lymm and Stockton Heath to the Runcorn Gas Works and Halton Road Wharf, just short of Runcorn's Delph Bridge (27 miles 4 furlongs.)

During this period most of the former Leeds & Liverpool Canal carriers gravitated to working around the Manchester Docks and the Bridgewater Canal, (these carriers were sometimes referred to as 'Jemmies). Albert Blundell, and Billy Wells, were there, even the aristocratic John Parkes & Sons' boats from Liverpool appeared when the Tate & Lyle, and Liverpool Gas Works traffic ceased.

The power station job however, as the boatmen all realised, could only last for a comparatively limited time; it was obvious that even the most modern of installations could only have a fairly short lifespan and would soon become obsolescent, although, because of its CHP contracts one of the oldest, Bloom Street, was to be an exception. Some experiments were made in the use of substitute fuels. One trial involved 'sea coal', 'salvaged' and loaded onto motor lorries on the sea-shore at Northumberland, then carried by road to the Trafford Park power station. Mr Monk describes the 'sea coal' as looking like 'duck-stones' (round cobble-stones used for paving), and reputedly it does not seem to have burnt much better, producing masses of clinker which welded themselves to the fire-bars.

A more serious threat came from an influx of coal, again carried by road motor in ten ton loads which the BEA purchased from the Yorkshire coal fields, and was said to be cheaper at the pit-head than that produced in Lancashire.

The British Electricity Authority claimed that, despite the long haul over the Pennines the overall cost was less than that of Lancashire coal carried by canal, a statement which the boatmen doubted as 'long boats' like Monk's *Burscough II* carried 80 tons, and the accompanying 62 ft dumb boat loaded 40 tons, that made 120 tons per trip, the equivalent of ten lorry loads, whilst the running time from Boothstown, over the Barton Swing Aqueduct and

Right) Rochdale Canal. 10 June 1968: The Rochdale Canal slipped tealthily through the centre of Manchester; leaving Castlefield at Duke's .ock, Monk boats heading for Bloom Street negotiated the Deansgate 'unnel, from the top of which this photograph was taken, the lock simply alled 'Tunnel'. The arches on the left supported the former Cheshire .ines Company's Central Station complex, a prominent feature being the ypical storage tank holding the locomotive water supply. Whitworth treet ran parallel to but above the towpath on the right of our picture. .ooking ahead, the next lock named Albion Mills is situated at the point vhere Albion Street crosses the canal and looking forward through the bridge hole' are seen the gates of the lock at Tib Street, known just as Tib" and unmistakable on the corner of Oxford Street with its 220ft lock tower the Refuge Assurance Building designed by A. Waterhouse nd extended in 1910 by P. Waterhouse. The next feature Jim Monk ecalls was the hospital complex appearing on the right-hand side, together vith the bridge crossing the canal at Oxford Street (or Oxford Road, the erms seem to have been used quite freely as the thoroughfares join end-on). The final lock to be surmounted on the 'coal run' was negotiated and the oats arrived at the Bloom Street Arm, where the Power Station to which im Monk Snr. and his sons carried washed singles and smalls commencing in the 1930's with horse-drawn boats) over several decades vas situated. Originally there were two arms (see Map page 35) Jim Monk remarks that the run was often referred to by the boatmen as the Dickinson Street" as "the Bloom Street" job. By 1804 four years after ne canal opened, T & M Pickford were running an express delivery service vith a fleet of fly boats from a base on the Lower Dickenson Street Arm s 'Bloom Street' was then known. The fly boats were smallish narrow oats with a draught of 2 ft 6 ins and a 20 ton capacity. There was also a varehouse, dry-dock and boat-building yard situated here; the names and pellings 'Dickenson' and 'Dickinson' even 'Dicconson' being used ccording to local custom and whim. ***Gordon Biddle***

along the Bridgewater Canal to Trafford Power Station was only 2½ hours as opposed to the long haul by road across the backbone of England.

At the turn of the century Trafford Power & Light Supply Ltd, were supplying electricity from an early generating station on the same site which the power station occupied in the 1950's. The TP & LS installation was purchased by the Stretford Urban District Council after World War I, and the Stretford & District Electricity Board was formed subsequently. Production ceased in the 1930's when the Central Electricity Board was formed, but the generating station was rebuilt in the early days of World War II, to be taken over by the British Electricity Authority on 1st April 1948.

During the years when the Monk boats were engaged on the 'coal job' up to 4,000 tons of boiler slack per week was ferried along the Leigh Branch of the Bridgewater canal - by all the carriers concerned - to the power stations. At Trafford Park it was discharged from the boats by means of flexible, moveable 7 inch diameter suction pipes, suspended from booms and discharging first into a receiver and thence by conveyor belt direct to the bunkers, (which had a 1,000 ton capacity) or alternatively was diverted to a stock pile, from which it would be recovered by a 'drag scraper' when required and transferred across the canal by overhead conveyor belt. The power station is now demolished and the former coal stockyard has became part of Manchester United Football Club's premises.

When Barton Power Station was in all-out production, with twelve of the fifteen boilers under full steam night and day, the demand for coal seemed insatiable, particularly in winter time. Barton was the Manchester Corporation Electricity Department's fourth power station and had been officially opened by the Earl of Derby on 11 October 1923, Dickinson Street having been the first, Bloom Street the second and Stuart Street, opened in 1902 the third. At peak periods in the 1950's an emergency request would often be received at a colliery around four-o'clock on a Friday afternoon, for 8 boats to be loaded and despatched on a Saturday morning, requiring special arrangements to be made as the tips did not always work at week-ends. Of course during the years of World War II all power stations had been under intense pressure with plants working day and night, this also meant 24 hour shifts on the bunkering plants and under the weak blue lights that were all that was permitted for obvious reasons, this was an extremely hazardous operation. All this besides 'Fire Watching' coping with the effects of the 'Blitz' and 'Home Guard' duties cheerfully undertaken by all members of the staff.

Jim recalls how enthusiastic the men on the Generating Plant were about their job, and their station, and proud of its ability to supply power to the National Grid, however those days are long gone and Barton Power Station, once known as the "Queen of the North" was decommissioned on 18 March 1974. Barton Power Station is thought to have handled the largest number of

Wigan Boatyard. c.1947/8. Monks', *Spica* was registered at Liverpool, as No 1454, indicating her inspection by the local authority and certification as meeting requirements for 'living aboard.' She is seen following re-painting and, even in monochrome, the painter and signwriter's skill is apparent. Primary colours were used, with the engine houses painted green, with gold lining, blocked and shaded lettering, the decks were orange and blue, picked out in red, that was also the colour of the bollards; the sides of the steel-hulled boats were painted black and those of the wooden boats tarred. Mayors have been highly respected boatbuilders and repairers, for generations, originally repairing coastal sailing vessels on the tidal River Douglas, moving to their present site on the old railway yard at Tarleton (where they are still flourishing) in 1926. In 1932, now a limited company, Mayor's took over the canal company's boatyard at Wigan, but from 1959 have concentrated on their Tarleton Yard. *L.Monk Collection*

Former entrance to Manor Lock. Latchford. 15 July 1989. The opening of the Runcorn & Latchford Canal in 1804/5, enabled the 'Mersey Flats' to avoid the difficult stretch of the river below Warrington. Construction of the Manchester Ship Canal destroyed whole sections of the R&L. However the length that became known as the Black Bear Canal, running from Manor Lock (formerly Latchford Lock) to Twenty Steps Lock (built at the same time as the new ship canal) formed a link between the MSC and the important Howley Quay Depot downstream (centre.) To the right is the spire of St Elphin's Church, and school (later at Darley Dale), for the daughters of clergy, where Richmal Crompton Lambourne, author of the 'William' stories was a boarder.

Norman Jones

Howley Quay. 11th June 1989. The 'modernised' building (left) is a reconstruction of a two-storey, three-bay, warehouse of 1850. The ground floor was open on all sides and the first floor enclosed, with a 25° double pitched roof over each bay and a 45° double pitched gable on the south face all still recognisable. The pulley bracketed out from the centre gable was not a hoist, but drove a horizontal travelling gantry. The companion building with its awning cantilevered out over the River Mersey was built about 1874 and that also boasted a travelling gantry, which ran from the front of the canopy to the back of the shed. When waterborne traffic finished, it was hoped that a Marina might be based here and for one or two seasons cruises were run from the Quay to the limit of navigation at Woolston Weir by small motor launches, a very pleasant jaunt, but the emphasis has now turned to 'on shore' entertainments.

Norman Jones

SOME OF THE BOATS - AND SOME OF THE MEN

June, a former Calder & Hebble barge, was purchased by Mr J. Monk Snr especially for the Manchester Ship Canal trade, for which she was ideally suited having a good turn of speed and long, deep keel which made for good handling in the busy waters of the 'Big Ditch', although her consequently deeper draught did cause some problems when traversing the badly silted Runcorn & Latchford Canal between Twenty Steps and Manor Locks where the boats turned left to go downstream into the River Mersey for Howley Quay.

A preserved and photogenic *June*, has now returned to her native waters after years of sterling service in the 'Monk' fleet and, carrying the square sail of a Yorkshire 'keel rig' and currently engaged in the 'tripping' business is a popular visitor to sundry waterway events. In 1992 she made a delightful picture at Sowerby Bridge, whilst supporting the campaign for the reconnecting of the Rochdale Canal and Calder & Hebble Navigation at that locale by removal of the blockage at Tuel Lane.

The fact that 'other carriers' played a significant role in handling Bridgewater and MSC trade indicates the volume of waterborne traffic in that halcyon period when Manchester was a major port. This too, at a time when the Ship Canal was also operating their own fleet of six motor barges, new to them in 1948, and all carrying the prefix 'Par', eg. *Paradine, Parbella, Parcastle, Parderry, Parelia* and *Parfield*, each capable of loading 70 tons, in addition to their towing capabilities.

One MSC owned motor barge of the 'Par' class usually towed two dumb barges, in 'v' formation on the Manchester Ship Canal, and in addition to lightening ships at Ellesmere Port they might also load at Liverpool or 'across the water' at Birkenhead

continued on page 46

Manor Lock, Swing Bridge. 11 June 1989. Originally the Latchford Lock of the 7¾ mile long Runcorn & Latchford Canal, opened in 1804, to provide a route to Runcorn, thereby avoiding the problems of the M&L navigation beyond the Howley Tidal Lock and the treacherous widening estuary beyond Warrington's' Bank Quay the name was later changed to avoid confusion with the new Manchester Ship Canal's Latchford Locks. That canal severed the R&L leaving operable only the short stretch from Twenty Steps Lock to Manor Lock and the River Mersey. The canal route from Stockton Heath to Manor Lock was unremarkable although now, as a linear park the section from Black Bear bridge is landscaped with tree-lined banks on the right and to the left lies the Victoria Park its further perimeter marked by the River Mersey, the weir and Howley Lock. The Mersey Development Corporation has landscaped both the route *(Page 61)* and the Manor Lock site, which is stopped off with steel piling. Although the lock site is in part filled in and grassed over, the gates, some winding gear, mooring bollards and, as illustrated a well preserved example of the type of swing bridge used throughout the Mersey & Irwell Navigation are preserved at Manor Lock and a pedestal mounted plaque regrettably frequently vandalised by graffiti, records the history of the site. ***Norman Jones***

(Right) Old Quay Swing Bridge, Manchester Ship Canal. 1948. This first of two photographs taken on Cooper's *Hopper No 8* shows the volume of traffic using the canal through which the Monk family, and Albert Blundell with their former Leeds & Liverpool short boats and their 72ft craft made their way between Manchester, Howley Quay, and Ellesmere Port. Air pollution was obviously not an issue and the Transporter and Railway Bridges are shrouded in haze and smoke from the Widnes chemical industries, steam coasters and other vessels. The Old Quay Swing Bridge (open left) led on the opposite bank to the desolate point of land defined by *Hempstone Point* and on the canal side of this area were the Wigg and C&M Works of Imperial Chemical Industries Ltd. Further upstream Randles Sluices, allow flood water to pass into the River Mersey, and Liverpool's supply of fresh water from Lake Vyrnwy passes beneath the ship canal. ***James Ashton***

(Below) April 1961. Having run the gauntlet of the ship canal from Ellesmere Port where they loaded aluminium ingots for Howley Quay, Mr Jim Monk Jnr. and Tommy Cullen work *Irwell* through Twenty Steps Lock onto the comparative seclusion of the Runcorn and Latchford Canal, *June* meanwhile being moored at the tail of the lock.
Norman Jones

continued from page 44

Docks, being especially equipped (similarly to Ainscough's barges), for these 'esturial' as well as inland waterway duties. The MSC also owned 19 dumb boats, all named after Cheshire meres or lakes and carrying 'mere' suffixes. One of the series, *Barmere*, which the author photographed in 1960 moored on the Runcorn & Latchford Canal alongside Albert Blundell's *Cadellis*, was one of a batch of six which came from W J Yarwood & Sons of Northwich, in 1948.

Statistically these craft also seem to have been 'oversize' (but this did not affect their ability to pass through Hulme Locks); dimensions quoted for the 'meres' were 71ft x 14ft 9ins, draught when fully loaded 5ft 5ins. *Barmere* has been restored for the Sankey Canal Restoration Society, whilst sister vessel *Bigmere* can be seen at the Ellesmere Port Boat Museum.

For various duties around the dock system, and to handle their dumb boats in the 1950's the MSC maintained the smart little lighterage tugs:

MSC Daphne	30 tons	*MSC Rochdale*	17 tons
MSC Dolphin	14 tons	*MSC Thelwall*	17 tons

Old Quay. MSC 1948. From the bridge of William Cooper & Sons, Cardiff registered steam *Hopper No 8,* (later re-named *Sifter*) 499 grt, 140ft x 33ft 2ins x 11ft 6ins, built by R Stephenson & Co Ltd at Newcastle-on-Tyne, 9-1905 is observed the MSC in its heyday. Left of the small coaster 'coming up' lies the Old Quay Workshops and Tying Up Berths. To the right, on the other side of the sea wall lies the wide expanse of the River Mersey at the aptly named 'Runcorn Gap.' and Old Quay Lock 250ft x 45ft, 13 miles from Eastham permitting access between Runcorn Docks, the canal and river, for smaller vessels. Thirteen years would elapse before the graceful Transporter Bridge, its towers and cables seen beyond the lock, a high level girder span on which ran a trolley, beneath which was a travelling platform carrying pedestrians, vehicles and animals, across river and canal and opened in 1905 was replaced by a road bridge and dismantled. Beyond the Transporter Bridge is the railway bridge carrying the Liverpool to London railway line, the bridge built by the L&NWR in 1869. ***James Ashton***

BRIDGING THE RUNCORN 'GAP'

Runcorn Railway & Transporter Bridges 4th Nov 1956. The Runcorn Ferry had been established for 700 years, and was the only means of crossing the estuary until the opening of the L&NW railway bridge in 1869 which included a footpath available to the public for a small fee. In addition to the approach viaducts there are three 305ft spans; a 75ft headway was stipulated for shipping. The platform of the 1905 built Road Transporter Bridge, which cost £130,000 and was maintained by Widnes Corporation, was 55ft long by 24ft wide, suspended by steel wire ropes from the bridge trolley running on tracks beneath the high girders, supported on four graceful towers. The crossing took 4 minutes, the maximum load was 12 vehicles and 300 passengers. The bottom of the car, controlled by a motorman on the platform was just 12ft above high water level. By the 1950's the scheduled 20 minute service was unable to handle the volume of traffic. The 'transporter was dismantled when the new road bridge was opened in 1961.

Norman Jones

Widnes and the estuary, is separated from Runcorn and the Canal by the 2,950ft sea wall, built in the tideway. Faced on both sides by 12 inch piles, it rises from a base of 22ft to 16ft at the top. Compensating for the intrusion on the river course an equivalent space was reclaimed on the Widnes shore. Two steam lighterage tugs are returning from towing barges between Liverpool and Manchester. First (Top) is Rea Towing Co, Ltd's *Yewgarth* 111 grt tons of 1913, 500 ihp followed (Bottom) by the 72 grt *Sedge Cock* (II) of The Liverpool Screw Towage & Lighterage Co 300 ihp built 1933 as the *Eccleston,* to the Screw Towage Co in 1953, sold 1960.

Norman Jones

Thelwall Ferry. MSC 1958. Ferries were adopted across the new canal for minor roads and footpaths, but there had been a ferry crossing of the River Mersey here since 1652. On the north bank stands the Pumping Station with overhead conduits leading to the settling lagoons. Negotiating traffic such as this was commonplace for the Monk boats working between Manchester Docks, Ellesmere Port and Howley Quay. The screw tug *MSC Stanlow,* 100 tons of 480 hp leading the *Carlo Martinolich* was built for the canal company in 1924 by W J Yarwood & Sons and sold 'Dutch' in 1965. Note that vessels pass 'port to port' and pounding along comes John Harker Ltd's *Wensleydale H*, displaying her 'hazardous cargo' flag. Of 256 grt, 157ft x 21ft 2ins x 8ft 6ins, she was built at Knottingley in 1947 and powered by a 6 cyl engine from the National Gas & Oil Engine Co, Ashton-under Lyne.
Norman Jones

Statham Pumping Station. MSC 1958. During the canal's construction bucket dredgers such as *Bollin* and *Irwell* were erected in partly excavated 'dry' channels and floated when water was admitted. However a dredging fleet was required when construction was completed as it was calculated that the rivers Mersey & Irwell as the watershed had a total length of nearly 300 miles and an acreage of 568,703, and that the normal flow of the Irwell at Manchester Docks would be 150,000,000 gallons daily, so the dredgers were constantly at working scooping up silt and other deposits to maintain the waterway at statutory depths. A fleet of thirteen tugs were at one time or another, assigned to the Dredging Department to haul the Hopper vessels of which *No 32* is a typical example. The Pumping Station was also served by the MSC railway. Over the years the material pumped into the lagoons has settled and part of the site is now the popular Woolston Eyes nature reserve.
Norman Jones

Thelwall, 1958. The Rome registered 'machinery aft' 6,170grt *Carlo Martinolich* 'in ballast' and owned by 'Fertilia' SPA thrashes past the pumping station, her stern held to the north bank by *MSC Sabre,* the first of the canal company's 'S' class of twin screw motor tugs of 147 tons that caused quite a sensation when they came out in 1956. They were of hydroconic hull design built by P K Harris (Shipbuilders) Ltd, at Appledore and featured a spacious wheelhouse with a clear view aft. The hull form facilitated manoeuverability, aided by two Ruston & Hornsby oil engines driving twin screws and developing 1,200bhp although purists might regret the replacement of a funnel by a tripod mast of which the port and starboard legs served as engine exhausts.
Norman Jones

In the 1960's the Bridgewater Department tugs were :

Appleton 21 tons
Baddeley 21 tons
MSC Bantam 1 Launch tug
MSC Bantam II Launch tug

When the partially lightened ocean going grain ships eventually reached Manchester Docks unloading continued on a 24 hour basis, by means of suction pipes suspended from the massive elevators which transferred the grain from the ships to on-shore storage hoppers beside Kellogg's Factory which was established beside the Bridgewater Canal in 1938.

In the latter 1950's about 100,000 tons of grain per annum was waterborne and discharged at Trafford Park by the pneumatic grain elevators. Amongst Monk's short-haul jobs were trips from Manchester Docks up the River Irwell to Castlefield, with enormous rolls of paper, or cases of tea, the latter emitting a mouth watering aroma; there were also deliveries to the Water Street Warehouse of general cargo for storage and/or transhipment, whilst some of the more exotic cargoes which Mr Monk recalls as being moved by barge were Mexican Hardwoods, North American Lead, Coir Fibre from India and Burmese Paraffin Wax.

Manchester lost many fine buildings during the 'Blitz' not least in the Castlefield area, which, in due course the Bridgewater Department replaced by less aesthetically pleasing but no less effective modern transit sheds. Here in the heart of the city at Castlefield, the Bridgewater Canal has its junction with the Rochdale Canal, the River Medlock, and the short 1/8th mile branch leading to the upper reaches of the River Irwell and the Hulme Locks. Nearby was the main road transport depot and Chester Road headquarters of the MSC's Bridgewater Department.

Burscough II was sometimes engaged on ship's husbandry duties, loading chandlery supplies (over a period of perhaps 2 days under tight security) at the Bonded Warehouse in Water Street, for delivery to ocean going bulkers discharging ore for the Lancashire Steel Corporation at Irlam Wharf on the MSC's northern bank. The works which was by then a part of the British Steel group closed in 1979. The vast site of the former complex with its internal railways and blast furnaces is now Irlam Northbank Industrial Park, and a part of the flourishing Trafford Park Development Area (UDA). The quays where the ore ships used to discharge are still extant.

On arrival at Irlam the *Burscough II's* cargo, which always included cases of whisky and crates of beer amongst the 'consumables' was unloaded by the ship's derricks, under the eyes of the freighter's Mate as the Monk boat lay alongside; meanwhile transference of ore from the main holds continued unabated, raising clouds of ochre coloured, abrasive dust, which coated the vessels and dockside and penetrated into every nook and cranny below decks. Despite all precautions at the bonded store pilfering sometimes occurred and Jim recalls the unpleasantness once when several crates of spirits were missing when the load was tallied off, leading to a worrying but indeterminate official investigation, which exonerated Monks' from any blame.

Other bulk loads were of sand, Hughie Martland one of Monks' regular skippers often worked as many as three boat loads every day, from a depot at Manchester's No.1 Pomona Dock adjacent to Cornbrook Road, to a concrete works at Trafford Park, whilst Bill Mayo, a Wigan man and former Canal Transport Company employee who became a Monk skipper was very experienced in dock work, in which the boats usually worked in pairs with a three man crew between them.

THE MARY P COOPER INCIDENT

'Coopers', (William Cooper & Sons Ltd,) with offices at 11 Rumford Street, Liverpool, established for over a century as suppliers of sand, gravel, and latterly concrete aggregates and ready mixed concrete also, had depots at Birkenhead, Liverpool, Manchester, at No 1 Pomona, mentioned in the previous paragraphs Warrington and Widnes. Their Warrington offices were situated in Greenall's Avenue, near the Manchester Ship Canal's Walton laye-by.

Coopers' not only had quarries at Gresford and Rossett in North Wales, but also dredged for sand 'over the Bar' in the Mersey Estuary, and a serious incident involving one of their vessels, whilst returning from one of these trips closed the ship canal to large vessels for some days, during which time the 'bye-traders' 72ft boats worked full stretch on the 'shuttle' services from Ellesmere Port.

It was at about 5.45pm on Tuesday evening the 21st March 1961 that Cooper's 1,000 ton, 65 years old steamer the *Mary P. Cooper,* proceeding from Eastham to Manchester with 900 tons of sand, having reached a point about 200 yards east of the Northwich Road Swing Bridge (at Stockton Heath, Warrington) was in collision with John S Monks & Co Ltd's *Foamville,* (1,150 dwt) bound for Ireland with a cargo of cattle food. The *Mary P. Cooper* received a fatal blow just beyond the stem on the port side and the port bow of the *Foamville* was also damaged, the vessels were attempting to pass correctly, port side to port -rather discounting the efficacy of the rhyme which every embryo helmsman learnt by rote "GREEN TO GREEN AND RED TO RED, PERFECT SAFETY, GO AHEAD." Rebounding from the shock of the impact the stern of the *Foamville* struck the steep, sandstone north bank of the canal, with an impact which severely damaged her rudder and propeller.

Hatch covers had not been secured on the *'Mary P'* and with her holds open the sand-hopper sank within five minutes. Local residents who had rushed from their homes on hearing the crash assisted a passing policeman; a rope and lifebelt were thrown, and the eight crew members who had jumped from the disappearing *"Mary P."* into the cold, murky waters of the canal were hauled up the steep bank to safety.

Skipper Harry Farmer was the last to leave the ship, but first courageously went down into the fast flooding engine room and opened the boiler escape valves, mindful of the danger to local residents should the boiler explode.

continued on page 54

Stockton Heath. *sv Dispenser* and Pontoons. March 1961. Having allocated ferry crossings over the new canal nine main roads required bridges. Those at Warburton and Latchford, the latter seen here were intended to be swing bridges, but powers were obtained to carry the roads over the canal on embankments and high level fixed bridges with a headway of 75ft. They are of Forth Bridge cantilever type with central spans of 206ft and side spans of 58ft. The roadway is 18ft wide with two footpaths 3ft 6in wide each side, 780 tons of steel were used in constructing each bridge. Beyond the cantilever bridge may be discerned the Knutsford Road Swing Bridge, one of the heaviest of the seven at 1,083 tons. Also in the scene is one of the five railway deviation bridges, with a clear headway of 75ft and beyond that Latchford Locks. Albert Blundell's *Cadellis* approaching bound for Ellesmere Port is hugging the north bank to keep clear of the 'O' class tug of which *MSC Onset,* a *tsmv* of 154 tons built by Henry Robb Ltd, with Crossley engines in 1947 was the first. ***Norman Jones***

At this time work on the sunken *Mary P. Cooper* is mostly being done underwater by the hard-hat divers, Albert Blundell, sitting on the cabin top views the site as *Cadellis* passes at slow speed. However the Admiralty vessel *sv Dispenser,* 775 grt, built by Smith's Dry Dock Co Ltd, 10 - 1943, and powered by a triple cylinder steam engine, is seen to already have two stout wires down to the wreck from her bow lifting gear *(right).* ***Norman Jones***

SS *Foamville* on the MSC Sept 1955. Although this photograph predates her encounter with the *Mary P. Cooper,* **(bottom at Latchford)** the *Foamville* has been assessed for bow damage the plates requiring attention marked in engineer's chalk. One plate is pierced at F16, and compression bruising at D13 is marked *. Such damage was often experienced by small coasters, which had to penetrate into small ports, or creeks with minimum facilities, and in all weathers, and in no way reflected adversely on the shipowners or the masters and crew of these invaluable 'maids of all work.' This single screw 869grt machinery aft vessel, 427t nett and 1140t deadwt Official No 146685, Call Sign MLGP, was built January 1923, by SH & SR Hansen & Co Ltd, Bideford. Former names were *Runnelstone* in 1946 and *Elgeiba* in 1954. Dimensions 190ft x 30ft 1in x 14 ft $1\frac{1}{2}$in. Triple-expansion engines 3cy. 16in, 27in & 44in x 30in were by MacColl & Pollock Ltd, of Sunderland, supplied with steam by two single-ended boilers pressed at 180 lb, natural draught. ***Ted Gray (left) and Jim Ashton (below)***

Twenty Steps. Stockton Heath c.1927. The Eastham Ferry, Pleasure Gardens & Hotel Co Ltd's 223grt *PS Sapphire* leaving the stage by Twenty Steps Lock with a 'day return' excursion to New Brighton, calling at Runcorn, Weston Point, Ellesmere Port and Eastham to pick up and set down. Originally buff with a black top by this time the funnel colours were, from the bottom, red, with a white band and blue top. The lock gates of the Runcorn & Latchford Canal can be seen beneath the bulk of the Northwich Road Swing Bridge, to the right of the picture. I believe that only a small numnber of trips operated this service over two or three seasons, what I do know is that, our Jones family went on all of them and I must have been in the stern of the *Sapphire* as she made her spectacular smoky, flip-flopping departure. There was a garden type seat placed squarely across the pointed stern, and this we commandeered, complete with packages of egg and corned-beef sandwiches and flasks of tea. It was a super day out.

David Fance

Northwich Road Swing Bridge. March 1961. Albert Blundell's *Cadellis,* Yarwood built MSC dumb barge *Ellesmere* and a *Par Class* motor await orders at the top of Twenty Steps Lock. During the construction of the Ship Canal the River Mersey's course was diverted by a cutting called the "New River." A dock was planned for Warrington but never built, although a wharf and travelling crane were provided where river and Ship Canal met. When the R&L Canal was severed where it crossed by the Northwich Road, the **TWENTY STEPS** fixed bridge was replaced by the swing bridge across the new canal and the lock built to connect the MSC & R&L canals took the name of the former bridge. A new lock at Walton gave access from the new Ship Canal to wharves at Warrington on the old Mersey & Irwell Navigation. Despite the severance of the R&L Canal an industrial water supply to Runcorn was maintained using some piped sections.

Norman Jones

Bridgewater Canal. Top Section. Runcorn Entrance Locks. 21 July 1961. The canal reached Lumbrook in 1770 and Stockton Heath in 1771. Here goods were transhipped, taken to Warrington and sent on to Liverpool by Mersey flats. The Duke had a Mansion built near Runcorn and in 1772 bought 200 bedsteads and mattresses, and put some of the workers building the new locks in his house and others in three hulks, which were also breakwaters for work at the lower locks. The ten pairs of staircase locks opened on 1 January 1773. Each fell 7ft, except the lowest, which fell 22½ft enabling use at any state of the tide. A second flight superseding these opened in 1827, left the original locks below the top pair and ran diagonally across the ends of the existing basins to an extension of the tidal dock, gaining the river via a pair of gates when the tide was suitable. Regrettably the flight was abandoned in 1966 and the site filled in.

H Arnold - Waterway Images

Stretford, 16 Jan 1962. Bound for Runcorn Gas Works, Mr J Monk Snr, steers *George* alongside the 'leccy'. The Manchester, South Junction & Altrincham Railway was formed in 1844 when the Manchester & Birmingham, together with the Sheffield, Ashton-under-Lyne, & Manchester Railway promoted an eight mile branch line, opened in 1849 from Manchester to Altrincham. This became an important commuter passenger line, and £900,000 was authorised to electrify the line on a 1,500 volt DC system that started on Monday, 11 May 1931, with electric trains working a 20 minute interval service from each terminus. The steel gantries, supported the overhead conductor wires at 16ft above rail level and were placed 220ft apart. The high voltage was as recommended by the 1927 Railway Electrification Advisory Committee. Today Metrolink trams plying between Altrincham, Manchester city-centre and Bury run beside the canal.

H Arnold - Waterway Images

Preston Brook Warehouse. 7 July 1957. 23 miles 3 furlongs from Waters Meeting Stretford, to Preston Brook Junc. South, on the T&M. is the 1,239 yard Preston Brook Tunnel. A converted 'Little Packet' lies beside the 5,000 ton capacity warehouse, in its day a transhipment point for traffic brought by broad-beamed craft from Liverpool via Runcorn Docks, or the Ship Canal and Manchester Docks, and narrow boats, south-bound to the Midlands and points beyond; also traffic via the Anderton Lift to the River Weaver and ICI. By 1957 the building served as a Maintenance Depot Store and its sale was being negotiated in 1997.

Norman Jones

Runcorn Gasworks. Saturday, 24 February, 1962. Monk's *George* is lying outside Albert Blundell's *Finch,* at the wide-open expanse of Runcorn Gas Works on the Bridgewater Canal. *George* was the 'converted' horse boat *(page 18)* that Mr James Monk Senior bought from Thomason's in the early 1940's. The differing styles of artistic paint work on the bows of both boats can clearly be distinguished, as can the single bollards on the Monk boats as opposed to the double fitting on Albert Blundell's *Finch.* Tanning was still an important industry at this time and the Astmoor, Highfield, Royal Oak and Camden Tanneries were all adjacent, whilst just beyond the Gas Works lay the former Runcorn Dock Yard known to boatmen as 'The Sprinch'. ***H Arnold Photography***

continued from page 49

All traffic on the MSC was immediately halted, but preparations for salvage began at once and continued night and day. For several days all traffic requiring to pass the scene of the collision was stopped, but as the divers and salvage men secured the wreck, first the *'Par'* class motor barges and their associated dumb boats, and the 72 foot boats of the 'bye-traders' and then small coasters were able to work past with care and at reduced speed; whilst 'awaiting orders' the motor barges were stationed on the Runcorn & Latchford Canal adjacent to the Twenty Steps Lock at Stockton Heath. As the work progressed large ships and tugs were allowed to pass the site using extreme caution.

The salvage work culminated in success on the morning of Sunday, 16th April 1961, when the final lift was initiated by the *SV Dispenser*, utilising four Admiralty pontoons and a battery of air compressors, the MSC's hard-hat divers having made good and sealed the hull of the wreck.

The following morning, suspended between pontoons the hulk was towed by the tugs *MSC Onset* (1948\154grt), *MSC Quest* (1952\144grt) and *MSC Dawn* (Dredging tug) back through the Northwich Road Swing bridge into the Walton laye-bye where she was to end her days, being eventually moved a few hundred yards from Naylor's timber wharf, where she was temporarily berthed and jettisoned in a disused creek at the end of the basin near Greenall's Avenue, to suffer over the course of time, the ignominy of being buried beneath hundreds of tons of rubbish as the creek was 'reclaimed.'

In addition to the *Mary P. Cooper* the firm of William Cooper's also owned a very interesting collection of mainly veteran steamers.

J.MONK & SONS - Fleet List:

62 FOOT SHORT BOATS, Wooden Construction
*Jean, Pauline**, *Kathleen, Sylvia, Marian, James, George, Ethel* and *Spica,* later renamed *Wilfred.*
The fore-going named,(excepting for *George*,)
After Members of the Family.

62 FOOT SHORT BOATS Iron Construction
Irwell, Weaver, Lune, Wye and *June.*

72 FOOT IRON BOATS
Burscough No 2, and *Boadicea.*
The *Sirius* which was repaired, altered and re-named *Pauline,* was purchased from the Canal Transport Company and is the boat that sank following the mishap at Bloom Street Power Station and was later replaced by a second *Pauline*.

TUGS

Two wooden tugs, named *Sulzer* and *Leo* bought from Messrs. J.Parkes & Sons Ltd, never worked in the Monk fleet, having been purchased to obtain the heavy duty Gardner Marine engines, by (Norris, Henty & Gardners Ltd, of Patricroft) with which they were fitted. The units were of two types, one a type 5LW with 4 1/4 inch x 6 inch cylinders (5) rated as 70 hp 1,300 rpm and the other of type 6LW with the same size of (6) cylinders rated 84 BHP also at 1,300 rpm The *Leo's* hull was broken up but that of the *Sulzer,* which had every nail made of copper was sold, as was the 5LW engine to a dealer in Yorkshire who specialised in shipping engines overseas, but the six cylinder Gardner was earmarked for installation in the Monks' own *Burscough II.* The Monk 'dumb' boats worked almost exclusively between Colliery Tips, the Power Stations and to Runcorn Gas Works, but when actively engaged in the Manchester Ship Canal trade, the power boats were to be found hard at work towing the MSC's 'Mere', class lighters.

BOATS AND ENGINES

When Mr J. Monk Snr bought the boat *June* from Goole, and brought her home to Adlington with Wilf, via the Aire & Calder Navigation and Leeds & Liverpool Canal, some modifications were needed before the she was ready to commence her new trade; the first job was to remove the deep coamings and replace them by shortened versions and also fit stanchions so that the holds could be sheeted up for dock work.

The 62ft motor boat *Irwell* also came from the Goole area, and as purchased was fitted with a life expired WIDDOP 24hp single cylinder engine; when Wilf and his Dad reached Leeds, they spent a couple of days replacing this engine, by another purchased from the Canal Transport Co.

Later, of course, Mr Monk bought Russell Newbery engines for some of their boats which Wilf fitted, helped by young Ernie Parkinson, and John Mailley who worked for the family for many years. The 6LW Gardner (ex tug) marine engine which they

Irlam Ore Wharf. MSC Mon, 29 June 1987. The immaculately turned out sludge disposal ship *Gilbert J. Fowler,* dressed overall, passes the now closed Steel Work's wharf bound for Eastham, carrying civic dignitaries on her last voyage along the canal before the base of operations was moved. This is the wharf to which Monk boats brought chandlery supplies. The Partington Iron & Steel Co. Ltd, was formed in 1910, a 109 acre site was purchased from the MSC and the Coke Ovens started up in 1913, in time for World War I! Originally ore was unloaded to rail at the MSC Eccles Wharf, but work on the 650ft long x 79ft 3 ins wide Wharf downstream of Irlam Viaduct, with a depth alongside of 30ft was completed and working by May 1932.

Norman Jones

Trafford Park. c1960. Skipper 'Hughie' Martland aboard *June,* moored at Kellogg's factory on Trafford Park, having arrived with a cargo of grain transhipped from vessels lying in Manchester Docks, is in the process of preparing a heap of rope for 'coiling down'. The neighbouring boat is of particular interest in that it is one of the barges equipped for working across the Mersey estuary, as witness the high coamings and steel hatch covers, as opposed to the cut-down coamings, and facilities for sheeting up, of the boats designed or modified for inland waters only. With hold and load exposed it is the next in turn to go under the suction intake pipes of the silo.

Norman Jones

Barton Power Station. 1950's. The 62ft wooden boat *James* is seen in pristine condition, with paintwork glistening in the the sunlight. The boats and Power Station have long gone, as have the collieries that fed them, but Trafford Park is still in business, with a flourishing Development Corporation established in 1987; between that date and 1995 over £1 billion of private sector investment has been attracted and there are over 1,330 companies in the Park employing about 43,000 people. ***L Monk***

Leigh Branch, Bridgewater Canal Nr. Worsley. 1950's. Having loaded to capacity at Boothstown, Mr J.Monk Jnr, steers an unidentified motor, and dumb boat in the direction of the Barton Aqueduct, Stretford Waters Meeting and Trafford Power Station. The breadth of the Duke of Bridgewater's vision in building his waterways to such dimensions that two 'broad' barges could pass without difficulty is evident in this low angle view. ***L Monk Collection***

reconditioned and fitted in the *Burscough II* ran so smoothly that a hexagonal threepenny piece could be balanced on the tappet lid cover, edge on, whilst the engine was running.

Two more Thornycroft engines were purchased, but were not without teething problems, despite the inherent excellence of the marque. They arrived fitted with shafts, propellers, and pump impellers of manganese bronze, a metal highly esteemed by marine engineers but unfortunately not so suitable for prolonged use in the enclosed confines of the docks and canals. Unfortunately the water was not only foul, but polluted with floating debris, and when the blades struck, for instance, a floating plank they bent.

The distorted blades and accompanying vibration, in turn caused the bearings to wear and stern shafts to run out of line, to such an extent indeed that their useful life was only for about eight to ten weeks. A local engineering firm made some steel shafts to Monks' special order, and Thornycroft suggested fitting cast-iron propellers to these. One of the latter type was tried on the *Jean,* but the blades shattered on impact with the floating debris; the problem was ultimately resolved by having steel propellers made to match the steel stern shafts.

An allied difficulty was a continual failure of the manganese bronze, water pump impellers. Owing to the chemical reaction of bronze to impurities in the water, which caused rapid corrosion, their life was only about three months and replacements cost £25.00 each, a considerable sum in the less inflated financial climate of that period. Some decades previously, similar difficulties with water soluble chemical pollutants attacking the hydraulic lifting rams, led to the Anderton Boat Lift being converted to electrical operation. Monks' resolved their problem by purchasing a small Jabsco pump for each Thornycroft engine, which Jim and Wilf fitted themselves and subsequently the engines and their installations were trouble free.

The family acquired such expertise in general maintenance, particularly of mechanical jobs, such as the routine fitting of engines, shafts and propellers, that complete assemblies could be dropped onto their beds, without recourse to crowbars and levering, all done ‘on the spot’ whilst contemporaries still called on the services of professional fitters.

An amusing story relates to a Russell Newbery engine which Wilf fitted to one of their boats whilst she was lying at Billy Wells' Stretford Boatyard. The three cylinder engine was originally fitted to Ainscough of Burscough's, *Boadicea,* and was a notoriously bad starter. As Mr Monk recalls, 'there were some big hefty men at Ainscough's' and it often took three or four of them, swinging in turns for an hour or so at a time to get the engine started for the day's work.

Jim remarked that there was no comparison between those massive, hand-start, heavily built commercial engines, with their beefy broad shelled bearings, requiring no small degree of physical effort, and know-how, to swing, and the (by comparison) lightweight units powering many of the present generation of canal cruisers.

Ainscough's had the Russell Newbery replaced by a four cylinder Leyland Comet, and Monks' bought the 3 cylinder 'Russell' for which they paid about £50.00 and took it to Stretford to fit in their 62 foot wooden short boat *Ethel*. Whilst they were hard at work, some of John Parkes' men came into the yard and questioned Wilf's chances of getting the engine to run, criticising his proven method of timing the valves by reference, to the sight glasses on the fuel pump. The same group were passing when the first trial was about to take place, and stayed to 'watch the fun' saying "You'll never get that thing to start". Without comment Wilf and fourteen year old Ernie Parkinson got 'on the handle' gave one good swing and the engine immediately sprang into healthy life, to the amazed admiration of the watchers.

Trafford Wharf. ND. The Wharf, as seen from the railway swing bridge, faced the open ends of Nos 6, 7 & 8 Docks. The CWS Ltd, Sun Flour Mills stood on Trafford Wharf Road, connected to the elevators and wharf by an enclosed bridge. The structure (left) bore two lines of lettering **SUN MILLS** and **ELEVATOR,** the final letters S and R can be seen. The second elevator served the TRAFFORD MILLS of Joseph Pyke & Sons. The nearer dumb boat is of the class that were worked across the Mersey estuary to Birkenhead, whilst on the bluff bows of the barge lying 'outside' unloading through a suction pipe appears the inscription **"FLY BOAT."** Further astern is a steam barge, behind that a working dredger, discharging spoil into a hopper barge alongside, and the master of the smart, yacht like steamer, has just 'blown' an obligatory warning blast as he approaches. ***Boat Museum Trust***

BOCM Wharf. 18 November 1974. Further downstream, between Trafford Wharf and the Manchester Dry Docks Co Ltd, was the British Oil & Cake Mills Ltd, wharf, where Cotton-seed, and cattle-feeding stuffs were handled. Former 'Monk' boats *Irwell* and *Wye* which had passed into the ownership of Apollo Canal Cruises of Shipley, for commercial and cruising use, were unloading grain collected for BOCM from Seaforth, Alan Holden is aboard *Wye,* whilst David Lowe exercises a watching brief on the quayside. *Wye* which cost about £850 in 1972, was re-engined and in 1979 received a new bottom, hatches, coamings and wheelhouse, winning a 'Best Working Boat' IWA trophy, but was sold and converted for pleasure use in 1982.
courtesy David Lowe

DOCK WORK/TOWING AND LIGHTENING OCEAN GOING CARGO LINERS. MANCHESTER DOCKS

Week Ending Saturday, 30 June 1956

Barge *Irwell*	Ex *Santa Madra*	To Kelloggs	101.10. 0
Barge *Irwell*	Ex *Santa Madra*	Overtime at Ship	3. 0. 0
Barge *Irwell*	Ex *Santa Madra*	Call out Kelloggs	7. 6. 0
Barge *Irwell*	Ex *Santa Madra*	Towing	6. 0. 0
Barge *Irwell*	Ex *Athens*	Maize	39. 0. 0
Barge *Irwell*	Ex *Athens*	Call out Kelloggs	3.12. 0
Barge *Irwell*	Ex *Athens*	Towing	3. 0. 0
Barge *Irwell*	Ex *Athens*	Lard, Tea, Board	66.15. 0

Total £230. 3. 0

July 1956

2nd	**Barge** *Irwell*	Lard, Castlefield to Kilverts	50 tons x 5/-d per ton	12.10. 0
5th	**Barge** *Jean*	Lead. Docks to Glovers	51 tons	12.15. 0
6th	**Barge** *Irwell*	Lead. Docks to Glovers	51 tons	12.15. 0
6th	**Barge** *Irwell*	Logs for Castlefield	29 tons x 8/-d	11.12. 0
9th	**Barge** *Irwell*	Maize.Docks to Kelloggs	52 tons x 5/-d	13. 0. 0
10th	**Barge** *James*	Linear Boards to W'gtn	51 tons x 8/-d	20. 8. 0
18th	**Barge** *Irwell*	Tea to Castlefield	48 tons x 5/-d	12. 0. 0

Total £95. 0. 0

1958
Ship: Ex *Manchester Miller*, to Warrington

Tues 5 May	**Barge** *June*	57tons
Tues 5 May	**Barge***Irwell*	56tons
Tues 5 May	**Barge***Ethel*	53tons

Paper ex Ship : *Ulefoss*
Salford to Warrington by *Irwell* 31tons
and Water Street to Warrington 55tons

= 252tons x 8/-d **Total £100.16. 0**

25 Aug	**Barge** *Sylvia*	Newsprint Dks to Worsley St.	50tons x 5/-d	12.10. 0
26 Aug	**Barge** *Irwell*	Newsprint as above	48tons x 5/-d	12. 0. 0
26 Aug	**Barge** *Sylvia*	Newsprint as above	51tons x 5/-d	12.15. 0
29 Aug	**Barge** *Irwell*	Aluminium Mchr toW'gton	56tons x 8/-d	22. 8. 0
29 Aug	**Barge** *Sylvia*	Paper. Mchr to W'gton	56tons 10cwt x 8/-d	22.12. 0

Total £82. 5. 0

1959
Ship : *Clan MacIntyre* visited 13/14/15 April

Barges *George, Ethel, Sylvia, June, Irwell and Marion*

	Lead to Glovers. 300tons x 5/-d	75. 0. 0
13 April	Overtime : *Ethel* 2 hours	10. 0
14 April	Overtime : *Sylvia, Marion,* 2 hours each	1. 0.0

Total £76. 10. 0

1964
Ship : Strick line's Khurzistan. Carge Maize.

26 May	**Barge** *Boadicea*	Docks - Kelloggs 64 tons	
27 May	**Barge** *Boadicea*	Docks - Kelloggs 64 tons	
28 May	**Barge** *Boadicea*	Docks - Kelloggs 64 tons	
		= 192T x 5/6d per ton	52.16. 0
27/28 May	8 hours overtime Kelloggs		3. 0. 0

Total £55. 16. 0

THE TOWING JOB

1964 Towing

21 April	*Ellesmere*	Salford - Ellesmere Port	3. 0. 0
23 April	*Alan Abbott*	Hulme Locks - Docks	0.10.0
23 April	*Linmere*	Docks - Kelloggs	1. 0. 0
24 April	*Linmere*	—do— and return.	2. 0. 0
25 April	*Linmere*	Kelloggs - Docks	1. 0. 0
27 April	*Linmere*	Docks - Kelloggs	1. 0. 0
28 April	*Bigmere*	Kelloggs to Docks	1. 0. 0
28 April	*Blakemere*	Rathbones to Docks	1. 0. 0
28 April	*Linmere*	Docks to Kelloggs	1. 0. 0

Total £11. 10. 0

1964

28 May	*Boadicea* towed *Hatchmere* and *Tableymere* Kelloggs to Docks	2. 0.0
28 May	*Boadicea* towed *Fred Abbott* Kelloggs to Hulme Locks	10.0
29 May	*Boadicea* towed *Colemere,* Docks - Hulme Locks	10.0
29 May	*Boadicea* towed *Hatchmere* and *Pickmere* Hulme Locks to Kelloggs	1. 0.0

Total £4. 0. 0

SHIPS STORES / CHANDLERY

1965

Water Street to Irlam Ore & Mineral Quays.

Mon 18 Jan.	*Boadicea* Loading and Journey	20. 0. 0
19/20 Jan.	Standing by waiting for ship. £8 per day	16. 0. 0

Total £36. 0. 0

24 Jan	Ships Stores, Pomona Dock to vessel *Husvick*	
	Boadicea, As arranged	10. 0. 0
	Overtime for two men as arranged.	10. 0. 0

Total £20. 0. 0

SUMMARISING SOME OTHER ENTRIES:

On the 4th, and 5th of March 1960 and the 6th which was a Sunday, *Wilfred* and *Sylvia* worked day and night unloading from the *American Press* and transporting grain to Water Street. A few days later *June* and *Irwell* were transhipping tea from the *Malabar* to the bonded warehouse at Castlefield. The early sixties were a busy time at the docks and four years later in 1964 the Monk boats were still hard at it, with *Boadicea* busily engaged on April 22nd in carrying Maize from the *Silverisle* lying at Ellesmere Port to Kelloggs at Trafford Park.

Worsley Boatyard, Drydock. Monday 17 July 1961. On the Leigh Branch north of the Barton Swing Aqueduct, and near Monton Green Bridge, either *Denise* or *Christine,* of Albert Blundell's fleet, (which Jim Monk recognises by the style and shade of paint applied to the back cabin) was under repair at a time when such MSC designated *"Water Carriers on the Bridgewater Canal and connecting Navigations"* still flourished. ***H Arnold - Waterway Images***

REPRISE

In July 1992, Mr Leonard Monk visited the Tarleton Boat Yard, where the Rufford Branch joins the River Douglas. Many old wooden boats have been scrapped here, after being floated out through the lock into the river, and set alight when aground at low water. Not all the charred remains have been washed out to sea by successive tides, and amongst the reeds at the river's edge, used by anglers as an extemporised fishing platform, Leonard identified the bottom planks of their short boat *Sylvia,* but nothing was left of Albert Blundell's *Finch,* or Dean Waddington's *Peter,* which were amongst the last L&L former 'coal boats' to be destroyed in this way at Tarleton.

There are still active 'boaters' at Tarleton however. Although Preston's Albert Edward Dock closed in 1980, the former Docklands have been sympathetically re-developed. The Preston Yacht Club and Preston Marina are housed in the dock, and although the old channel running from the Gut landfall buoy at sea, to Lytham has silted and now dries to a lesser depth than before it is still partly marked, and is navigated by some competent skippers, whilst sea going craft based at Tarleton, Lytham, Freckleton, and Hesketh Bank, do undertake the passage; vessels from Preston and the Marina visit around, and the river and estuary can be cruised without vessels actually going to sea. A comprehensive information pack is available from Suzanne Cameron at Preston Marine Services Ltd, Navigation Way, Ashton-on-Ribble, Preston PR2 2YP.

The boats of the 'bye-traders' and No 1's were always well maintained, and Monks' upheld those traditions, with a colour scheme using bright primary colours, with the engine houses painted green with a gold braid (or lining) round the edge, decks orange and blue, picked out in red, which was also the colour chosen for the bollards. The sides of steel hulled boats were painted black, and those of the wooden boats tarred.

As the waterway era drew to a close 'Monk's of Adlington' disposed of their boats and turned their attention to road haulage, becoming well known in transport circles, particularly in the Wigan/Preston area, operating a fleet of five, splendid twin-steer, 32 ton Foden articulated vehicles, the tractor units fitted with Gardner or Cummins engines; nor was their connection with shipping circles severed as they carried extensively for Northern Ireland Trailers then based at Preston Docks, latterly operating as PANDORO from Fleetwood, as part of the P&O Group.

continued on page 63

Twenty Steps Lock. 20 March 1961. *Irwell* has locked up from the Ship Canal and Jim Monk re-fills the lock for *June,* then both boats will proceed along the Runcorn & Latchford canal to Manor Lock and Howley Quay. ***Norman Jones***

Trafford Park. c.1952. Skipper Hughie Martland in characteristic pose, leans on *June's* tiller working on the 'grain job' unloading at Kellogg's Factory. In the background the hold of the next boat to go under the elevators has been uncovered. An interesting feature is *June's* 'ship size' engine-room ventilator cowl. ***L.Monk Collection***

April 1961. Stockton Heath. A week-end lay-over at Twenty Steps lock on the Runcorn & Latchford canal, the boat's crews having gone home until Monday morning, leaving the vessels without any qualms as to their safety in that less vandal prone decade. On parade are: Albert Blundell's *Cadellis,* (right) a Par class MSC 'motor' (centre) and her two 'dumb' boats *Bigmere* (extreme left) and astern of her, out of the picture *Ellesmere.* ***Norman Jones***

Howley Quay. 15 July 1989. Still in excellent condition is the former Agent's House built in the second decade of the last century, now complete with port and starboard 'running lights' as The Old Quay Tavern. On either side may be seen some of the warehouse buildings and there is access to the Quayside. The upper reaches of the river towards Woolston are very attractive. ***Norman Jones***

The Blackbear Linear Park. Over the years houses had encroached on the area surrounding the waterway and vandalism, dumping of rubbish and complaints from householders on the score of 'danger' led to the infilling of the canal in the mid seventies. The bridge carried the now closed former L&NW Warrington to Altrincham and Manchester railway line across the canal. ***Norman Jones***

R&L Canal. Blackbear Warehouse. 15 July 1989. The semi-circular pediment above the bricked in door-fittings indicates the one-time attachment of the open roof which covered the quay, that commenced where the bushes now grow whilst a heavy sliding door gave access to the mill/warehouse. ***Norman Jones***

Manor Lock. 15 July 1989. Over several decades Jim Monk Snr, and his sons Jim Monk Jnr. and Wilfred, had joined generations of boatmen in wearing down these steps dating back to the inception of the R&L Canal. The picture shows the remains of a winding mechanism similar to that in use on Page 19. ***Norman Jones***

THE MSC TODAY AND A 'RIGHT ROYAL OCCASION'

The arrival of shipping conglomerates, their absorption of long established liner and tramping companies and the construction of ever larger container vessels hastened the decline of Manchester Docks. Some traffic continues as far as Mode Wheel but it is pleasant to report that the western end of the canal is thriving. However on 7 March 1989 the MSC leased its four remaining 'V' Class twin screw tugs, to Carmet Tugs Ltd, who arranged to base them at Eastham on the ship canal so that they could be re-called to their former duties should the need arise. Complementary to the developments in what was once Dockland, the centrepiece of a new northern link into Trafford Park, joining the M602 motorway with the heart of the 'Park' and the first opening bridge to be built over the Ship Canal in 100 years was commissioned by Trafford Park Development Corporation following discussions commenced in 1990; at first a Double-Bascule bridge was considered, then an orthodox Swing Bridge, but the final decision was for the present design of low level vertical lift bridge, allowing 75ft air draft. Construction began in November 1992, and necessitated the demolition of a large office block which stood between the Proctor & Gamble and Cerestar buildings.

(Top left) Ellesmere Port. 23 Sep 1996. 13,000 whole timber piles form the embankment between the canal and river, seen beyond the smart Istanbul registered *Khoms* unloading Soda Ash from Bulgaria. ***A.J.Robinson***

(Top right) Eastham. 23 Sep 1996. The Carmet leased tugs, *MSC Viceroy, Victory, Viking* and *Volant* 130grt, 1,200 bhp were built by James Cook Ltd, (now sadly defunct) at Wivenhoe between 1974 and 1976. ***A.J.Robinson***

(Centre left) The appropriately named *Centenary Bridge* has a span of 41 metres, and a lift of 16 metres, the height of the platform above water level when raised is 23 metres. As completed the bridge is said to be the largest of its type in the United Kingdom. ***Keith Hodgkinson***

(Centre right) 1993. A replica of Drake's *Golden Hinde* shares the waters of the former No 8 Dock with radio controlled yachts. ***Ted Gray***

(Bottom left) Centenary Bridge, Trafford Park Thursday. 1st December 1994. Her Majesty, the Queen, accompanied by the Duke of Edinburgh performs the opening ceremony of the new bridge before an enthusiastic gathering of officials and others involved with the developments which have revitalised the area. ***Keith Hodgkinson***

The first Preston-Larne sailing was under the aegis of (Lt Col) Frank Bustard's Atlantic Steam Navigation Co, (later Townsend Thorenson, P&O *et.al*) whose chartered LST (landing ship tank) made the inaugural sailing of the new commercial ferry service from a 'Mulberry' pontoon installed on the site of the old cattle lairage at Preston Docks on Friday, 21st May 1948.

Geoffrey Wheat (author of Leeds and Liverpool Canal Craft 1972) purchased *Irwell* from Monks, and his colleague Derek Bent got *Weaver,* and in December 1972 Apollo Canal Cruises bought *Wye*. She cost about £850 and the intention was to use her for carrying and Camping cruises in the holiday season. Mr David Lowe Managing Director of Apollo Cruises has kindly made available some details of her career from which the following are highlights, not forgetting that the boats were also engaged in Camping Cruises in between-times:

Friday, 30 March 1973 - 23T coal Doncaster to Skipton.
Tuesday, 17th April 1973 - 26T steel Leeds to Liverpool (in conjunction with Irwell).
17th September 1973 - 60T Pipes (Local traffic) loaded at Field Locks, (Nos 16, 17, 18).
21 March 1974 - 32T stone, Gargrave to Esholt.
25 April 1974 - 10T Effluent, Shipley to Goole.
27 August 1974 - 39T Pipes, Nottingham to Esholt.

In October, November and December 1974, *Wye* was again engaged in the grain trade, transporting 30T loads from Liverpool to BOCM at Selby and also from Whitley Bridge on the Aire & Calder and from Liverpool to the BOCM Quay opposite No.9 Dock on the Manchester Ship Canal at Salford.

The activities of former Monk boats in service with Apollo Cruises have from time to time been recorded in text and illustration in the pages of the magazine Waterways World, and particularly with their journeys with sand, gravel and limestone on the River Soare and Sheffield & South Yorkshire Navigation. In 1973 Apollo fitted a replacement engine to *Wye,* but this was not satisfactory and a 4 cylinder BMC conversion was installed in 1974. During late 1979/1980 *Wye* underwent extensive repairs and refurbishment, being fitted with a new bottom, hatches, coamings and a very smart wheelhouse, and subsequently won the 'Best Working Boat' section, (Alfred Ritchie Trophy) at the Inland Waterways Association Rally held at Leeds. *Wye* was sold in 1982 for conversion to a pleasure craft at Doug Moore's yard at Barnoldswick.

Mr J.B.Barber, (J.B.Barge Co) who was one of Apollo Canal Cruises Directors purchased *Burscough II* from Monks c.Feb 1975 and in the April following put her to work on the grain run, working between Liverpool and Manchester. By this time passage of the Leeds and Liverpool Canal was becoming increasingly difficult for

On 'The Plough' Adlington, September 1971. When the Monk brothers became road hauliers rather than 'carriers by water' the nearby port, owned by the Borough of Preston and operated by the Preston Port Authority was the second largest municipal port in Britain, and the handsome Foden vehicles operated by JAMES MONK & SONS were a familiar sight at the North side container terminal, Albert Edward Dock, with *'NORTHERN IRELAND'* and later *FERRYMASTERS* trailers.

Monk Family Archives

August 1983. In its turn *Ferrymasters* came under the *PANDORO* banner and with the crossed P&O flag logo on the cab-front and trailer, Foden LTB 243 P, with the 250 hp Cummins engine takes centre stage.

Leonard Monk

working boats to negotiate and during one trip *Burscough II* picked up a load of wire on the propeller, which wound itself so tightly around the shaft that it needed British Waterways (whose help was invaluable) to de-water a short pound near Wigan so that the tangle could be removed. Unfortunately a leak was sustained as a result of this incident, and as re-bottoming was not a financially viable solution in view of the minimal amount of carrying work available, and the fact that the MSC then withdrew the boat's certificates *Burscough II* was disposed of and *Wye* returned to Yorkshire to work in the deeper waters of the Aire & Calder.

Burscough II was purchased from Mr Barber in May 1976 by Paul and Jean Doran, of Shannon Harbour, Eire where she arrived the following month, and was converted to the requirements of her new owners (see illustrations) at Kilalloe. Now based at Shanon Harbour, Co.Offaly, she is affectionately known to all and sundry just as *'the Liverpool Boat.'*

On 4th May 1991 Mr J.Monk Jnr and son Leonard visited the Booths Hall Basin near Worsley, where many old canal craft had sunk (or been sunk) when commercial carrying ended on the Leeds & Liverpool and Bridgewater Canals. The basin was to be drained in connection with redevelopment of the area for residential and recreational use. Of the hulks exposed to daylight Mr Monk, who he thinks he was probably amongst the last of the 'old guard' to have loaded at the basin, identified Albert Blundell's *Tom* and Dean Waddington's *Frank.*

Mr J.Monk Jnr. relinquished his haulage interests in 1987 but his elder brother Wilfred continued with his business activities until his sudden death after a very short illness at the age of 70 years on the 18th November 1993 . Wilf is greatly missed by his family and wide circle of friends by whom he was held in the highest esteem and this account of **J. MONK & SONS - LANCASHIRE CANAL CARRIERS,** is dedicated to his memory.

Burscough II's* interior** has been skilfully adapted for gracious living, this picture shows the saloon interior looking forward to the galley/ dinette area. ***courtesy Jean & Paul Doran

Shannon Harbour, Co. Offaly, Eire. July 1994. Although converted for living aboard, *Burscough II* is still a navigable craft and Paul Doran reports that her engine 'starts at the touch of the button'. The original hatches have been raised to form the roof of the saloon. ***courtesy Jean & Paul Doran***

Booths Hall Basin, Nr.Worsley. 4 May 1991. Amongst other abandoned craft the hulk of Dean Waddington's *Frank,* the name still distinct, was exposed when the basin was drained by developers. ***L.Monk***

Harry Mayor's Boatyard, Tarleton. August 1992. The remains of Monks' 62ft wooden short-boat *Sylvia* in use as a fisherman's platform on the banks of the River Douglas. ***L.Monk***